The
Our Father

A Guided Discovery for Groups and Individuals

Kevin Perrotta

LOYOLAPRESS.

CHICAGO

LOYOLAPRESS.

3441 N. ASHLAND AVENUE
CHICAGO, ILLINOIS 60657
(800) 621-1008
WWW.LOYOLABOOKS.ORG

Nihil Obstat
Reverend Jeffrey S. Grob, STL, JCD
Censor Deputatus
May 3, 2007

Imprimatur
Reverend John F. Canary, STL, DMin
Vicar General
Archdiocese of Chicago
May 4, 2007

The *Nihil Obstat* and *Imprimatur* are official declarations that a book is free of doctrinal and moral error. No implication is contained therein that those who have granted the *Nihil Obstat* and *Imprimatur* agree with the content, opinions, or statements expressed. Nor do they assume any legal responsibility associated with publication.

Unless otherwise noted, the Scripture quotations contained herein are from the New Revised Standard Version Bible: Catholic Edition, copyright © 1993 and 1989 by the Division of Christian Education of the National Council of the Churches of Christ in the U.S.A. Used by permission. All rights reserved. Subheadings in Scripture quotations have been added by Kevin Perrotta.

The excerpts from Romano Guardini (pp. 13 and 21) are taken from *The Lord's Prayer*, trans. Isabel McHugh (Manchester, NH: Sophia Institute Press, 1996).

"Surprised by His Father," by Fio Mascerenhas, SJ (pp. 25–27), is reprinted from *Pentecost Today*, January–April 2004. Used with permission of the author.

The excerpts from St. Teresa of Ávila (pp. 34, 44, 56, 78) are taken, with slight modifications, from *The Way of Perfection*, trans. E. Allison Peers, at ccel.org.

"Trusting the Father," by Marie Céres Marcelus (p. 49), is reprinted with permission of Louise M. Perrotta.

"Saved by the Our Father," by Helen Bloodgood (pp. 60–61), is used with her permission.

"Final Prayer," by Cynthia Cavnar (p. 83), is used with her permission.

Interior design by Kay Hartmann/Communique Design
Illustration by Anni Betts

ISBN-13: 978-0-8294-2167-5; ISBN-10: 0-8294-2167-X

Printed in the United States of America
07 08 09 10 11 12 Bang 10 9 8 7 6 5 4 3 2 1

Contents

How to Use This Guide

If you want a prayer to help you pray, the best one to begin with is the prayer that Jesus taught his disciples to pray—the Our Father, or Lord's Prayer. And if you want to deepen your understanding of the Our Father, a slow, careful reading of the prayer and of related Scripture passages is a good way to proceed. That is just what we are going to do in the present book. The goal of our reading is to grow in prayer by learning from the great model prayer that Jesus has given us.

Our approach will be a *guided discovery*. It will be *guided* because we all need support in understanding Scripture and reflecting on what it means for our lives. Scripture was written to be understood and applied in the community of faith. We read the Bible *for* ourselves but not *by* ourselves. Whether we are reading in a group or by ourselves, we need resources that aid in understanding. Our approach is also one of *discovery*, because each of us needs to encounter Scripture for ourselves and consider its meaning for our life. No one can do this for us.

This book is designed to give you both guidance for understanding and tools for discovery. You can use it in a group or alone.

The introduction on page 6 provides background material and helps you to get oriented for our exploration of the Lord's Prayer. A brief "Background" section in most of the weekly sessions will put the Scripture readings in context, and the "Exploring the Theme" section that follows the reading will bring out their meaning. Supplementary material between sessions will offer further resources for understanding and reflection.

The main tool for discovery is the "Questions for Reflection and Discussion" section in each session. The first questions in this section will spur you to notice things in the text, sharpen your powers of observation, and read for comprehension. The remaining questions suggest ways to compare the people, situations, and experiences in the biblical texts with your own life and the world today—an important step toward grasping what God is saying to you through the Scripture and what your response should be. Choose the questions you think will work best for you and your group.

Preparing to answer all the questions before your group meets is highly recommended.

We suggest that you pay particular attention to the final question each week, labeled "Focus question." This question points to some especially important issue raised by the reading. You may find it difficult to answer the focus question briefly. Do leave enough time for everyone in the group to discuss it!

Other sections encourage you to take an active approach to your Bible reading and discussion. At the start of each session, "Questions to Begin" will help you break the ice and start talk flowing. These questions are usually light and have only a slight connection to the reading. After each Scripture reading, there is a time for each person to offer a brief "First Impression." This is a chance to express an initial, personal response to the text. Each session ends with a "Prayer to Close" that suggests a way of expressing your response to God.

How long are the discussion sessions? We've assumed you will have about an hour and twenty minutes. If you have less time, you'll find that most of the elements can be shortened somewhat.

Is homework necessary? You will get the most out of your discussions if you read the weekly material and prepare your answers to the questions in advance of each meeting. If participants are not able to prepare, read the "Exploring the Theme" sections aloud at the points where they appear.

What about leadership? You don't have to be an expert in the Bible to lead a discussion. Choose one or two people to act as discussion facilitators, and have everyone in the group read "Suggestions for Bible Discussion Groups" (page 84) before beginning.

Does everyone need a guide? a Bible? Everyone in the group will need their own copy of this book. It contains the biblical texts, so a Bible is not absolutely necessary—but each person will find it useful to have one. You should have at least one Bible on hand for your discussions. (See page 88 for recommendations.)

Before you begin, take a look at the suggestions for Bible discussion groups (page 84) or individuals (page 87).

Have you ever had this experience? For some reason, you get to church well before Mass begins. The church is almost empty, and you break your normal pattern and sit up front. Gradually, people filter into the pews behind you, but you don't pay much attention to them. Mass begins. The congregation murmurs the responses in a subdued way. But when it comes time for the Our Father, you suddenly realize that the church is full of people, for everyone is praying the prayer quite loudly. Even little children can be heard, reciting it in their high, clear voices. The Our Father is obviously the part of the Mass with which everyone feels most familiar and most comfortable praying aloud.

Among all Christians, it seems, the Our Father is the most used and most cherished prayer. Many of us cannot remember when our parents taught us this prayer—or even if they taught it. We seem always to have known it. The prayer is a part of us.

Not only is the Our Father our first prayer in childhood. For some of us, it will be our last prayer in this world. Already some among us are sufferers of mental deterioration, who can no longer carry on a meaningful conversation but can still pray the Our Father without a hitch, as soon as someone else starts it.

You might wonder whether anything is to be gained from exploring such a familiar prayer. It may even be asked whether exploration is appropriate. After all, the Our Father is a *prayer*. The essential thing is to pray it, not talk about it. Discussion could be distracting.

Yet the Our Father is not only *a* prayer. It is a *model* prayer—a pattern for prayer. Introducing it, Jesus does not say, "Pray this prayer," but "Pray this way." He presented the prayer to us as a *lesson* in prayer. Some Christians, in fact, have spoken of the Our Father as a whole school of prayer—a school from which we never graduate, even in a lifetime. Thus, in addition to being prayed, the Our Father is to be pondered. No matter how thoroughly familiar we are with it, the Lord's Prayer contains depths we have not yet plumbed, lessons we have not yet mastered.

In this book we will read the Our Father slowly and carefully, along with a few other texts in Scripture that shed light on its meaning. As we go forward, we will repeatedly consider some important questions about this seven-petitioned prayer:

- What are we asking God for?
- What are we committing ourselves to?
- What picture of God do we imply by what we say to him in this prayer?
- What picture of ourselves do we imply?
- What does this model of prayer teach us about how to pray?

These will be the main lines of our exploration and reflection.

Beginning on the following page—before our first session—there is an introduction that examines the setting of the Our Father in Matthew's Gospel. Then, in Week 1, we will consider the prayer's address to God as Father. In Week 2, we will explore the first three petitions—our appeals that God's name would be hallowed, that his kingdom would come, and that his will would be done. In Weeks 3 through 6, we will explore the four remaining petitions of the prayer one by one.

To return to the Lord's Prayer is to return to the Lord who taught it. Exploring the prayer anew is an opportunity to become like a little child, asking Jesus once again to teach us how to pray. "Whoever does not receive the kingdom of God as a little child will never enter it," Jesus tells us (Luke 18:17). However much we have prayed, we remain infants, needing help to take our first steps. Indeed, only when we realize this are we getting somewhere in prayer!

Three Ways of Getting Close to God

The Context of the Our Father in Jesus' Sermon on the Mount

The Gospel writers have handed on to us two versions of the Lord's Prayer. St. Luke has given us the shorter version (Luke 11:2–4), St. Matthew the longer one (Matthew 6:9–13). This longer form is the one that we usually pray, and it is this form of the prayer that we are going to explore in the present book. In preparation for our exploration, it is helpful to view the prayer in its context in Matthew's Gospel. The prayer is located in the center of Jesus' great Sermon on the Mount (Matthew 5–7). In a sense, all of Jesus' instructions in the sermon about how we should live revolve around the Lord's Prayer, where we find ourselves alone with God.

In the opening of his sermon, Jesus calls us to purity of heart, that is, to a single-minded commitment to seek what pleases God (5:8). He commends those who hunger and thirst for justice (5:6). He tells us to follow God's law not in a merely external way but from the heart, in our thoughts and intentions, taking God himself as our standard of faithfulness, truthfulness, and love (5:1–48). Later in his sermon, Jesus cites the Golden Rule—"Do to others as you would have them do to you" (7:12). He urges us to go through the narrow gate that leads into the kingdom of God (7:13–14).

All of this is very demanding. Responding to this call requires deep personal change. But what can produce such a profound inner transformation? Where can we get the power to live this way? We know from our experience that our ability to change ourselves is rather limited. Remaking ourselves into people who always prefer God's will to our own seems beyond our reach. To love other people as we would like them to love us seems impossible, even in relationships of mutual trust and respect. Demonstrating God's love to those who have hurt us or threaten us often exceeds what we even aspire to.

Matthew's Gospel shows us that the source of personal transformation is Jesus himself. He is "God is with us" (see Matthew 1:23). He has come to forgive our sins and heal us of the sinful tendencies that lead us away from God. By his death and resurrection, Jesus reconciles us with God and gives us the inner freedom to respond to his call to perfection. The answer, then, to our questions about how we could ever respond to Jesus' challenging call is this: become his disciples. As Matthew shows, Jesus invites each of us to become one of his followers. In this discipleship relationship, through Jesus' personal presence and training, we can learn to imitate him in the circumstances of our own lives.

But this raises a further question. How can *we* respond to Jesus and become his disciples in the circumstances of our lives? We don't live in Palestine in the year 30. We can't walk along with him and his first followers on the roads of Galilee, observing his miracles, listening to his teaching, sitting around a table and having a conversation with him.

In the central section of his Sermon on the Mount (6:1–18), Jesus provides some answers to this question. He speaks about three means of being in contact with him and with his heavenly Father, three ways of responding to his spiritual presence and growing in relationship with him. The three means were already traditional in Judaism in the time of Jesus: acts of mercy, prayer, and fasting. Jesus presents them to us as means by which we can get close to him as his disciples. Let us look at this section of the Sermon on the Mount more closely (the biblical text is given on pages 17–18).

At the outset, Jesus identifies an issue that arises in all three of these kinds of religious behaviors. "Beware of practicing your piety before others" (6:1). All three types of piety have a public aspect, inasmuch as—immediately or eventually—our actions become known by other people. Others almost inevitably will find out when we help someone in need. Others see when we pray with the community of faith. And our fasting, too, often becomes known to others. But since the essential purpose of these activities is to grow closer to God, the public knowledge of our behavior gives rise to a danger. It opens the possibility of a different motive creeping in beside our desire to get close to God. The desire to gain other people's respect, approval, and admiration can become our main, if hidden, intention.

Almsgiving: 6:2–4. "Whenever you give alms . . ." (6:2). Our English word *alms* comes from the Greek word that is used here in the text of Matthew's Gospel. The New Revised Standard Version translates the word as "give alms." The English word *alms* implies giving money, but the Greek word is not so narrowly focused. Rather, it means showing mercy in any way. It encompasses not only financial giving but also any act of helpfulness, any expression of kindness, any form of aid to someone in need, any compassionate deed. We might paraphrase Jesus' words as "Whenever you show . . ."

Jesus' advice regarding acts of mercy boils down to this: do it for God's sake. In practice, this means doing it in a way that points people's attention to God. Our acts of compassion should enable people to see that *God* is their primary benefactor; we are simply the means he is using to show his love. We should give aid in a way that draws attention to God's generosity and brings him praise. "Let your light shine before others, so that they may see your good works and give glory to your Father in heaven" (5:16).

The description Jesus gives of those who act "to be seen by them" (6:1) contains the Greek word that has given us our English word *theater*. In a sense, Jesus is reminding us that our acts of kindness are necessarily a type of performance, for which there is always an audience. The questions he wants us to ask ourselves are these: When I show kindness, who is the audience for whom I am performing? Is it God? Or is it other people? Am I trying to show God how much I love him? Or am I trying to show other people how much I love God? And if I'm trying to show people how much I love God, how much *do* I love him? And, if I am mainly concerned that people would know that I love them and would thank me for it, am I acting out of love for them—or for myself? And a further question: If I am so keen on getting people's approval, why is their approval worth so much to me? Do I really need it so badly?

Jesus speaks of "the hypocrites" (6:2). The Greek word here means "actors in a play." The hypocrites whom Jesus describes act pious in public to gain other people's praise. By this very fact, their piety is false. They are pretending to love God. Perhaps their performance convinces other people; perhaps it even convinces themselves. But God isn't fooled.

If we put ourselves in the center of the picture, seeking to gain praise for our generosity, we distract people from God. Yet he is the original source of any help we provide. Jesus tells us that if we act this way, we shouldn't expect anything from God in return. Why should God reward us for leaving him out of the picture?

It is notable that Jesus does urge us to seek a reward from God. Act in such a way, Jesus says, that "your Father . . . will reward you" (6:4). Jesus is not suggesting that our acts of kindness place God under an obligation to us. God does not pay wages for services rendered. The reward that Jesus means is a deeper relationship with God.

Jesus does not speak here explicitly about acting out of genuine love for our neighbor. He implies, however, that showing kindness in order to please God is the essential basis for true love of neighbor. The reason is that the more we focus on pleasing God, the less we focus on trying to get something from those we serve. The attempt to please God frees us from the selfish desire to get something from other people—recognition, honor, praise—as payment for our kindness to them.

Jesus' discussion about showing mercy challenges us to examine our picture of God. If I regard the acclaim of other people as more important than God's approval, is it because God seems unimportant or unreal to me? If desiring to please my Father in heaven is not my motivation, is that because I do not think of him as my Father? Do I, instead, think of God as a distant deity, someone who deserves respect but not love? That is certainly not Jesus' picture of God.

Prayer: 6:5–8. By placing almsgiving first in his discussion of pious practices, Jesus indicates that growing closer to God involves loving and caring for other people. By putting prayer second, Jesus does not suggest that prayer is of secondary importance. Rather, he places prayer at the center of his instructions about pious practices, indicating that prayer is at the heart of merciful deeds and self-renunciation. By putting prayer at the center, Jesus implies that we can live his way of life only with God's help, obtained through prayer. Spending time in prayerful attentiveness to God is the starting point for coming to share God's desires for human lives and for society and to find the grace to cooperate.

Jesus' initial concern with prayer is the same as his concern with compassionate activities: we should pray to please God, not to impress other people (6:5–6). If we pray in order to be seen by other people, our prayer is valueless. It is valueless because, in fact, it is not prayer. Self-promotion is not prayer.

Jesus says of hypocrites, "They *love* to stand and pray . . . at the street corners, so that they may be seen by others" (6:5; italics mine). Hypocrites *enjoy* showing off. In their concern about what others think of them, they are concerned about themselves. For them, Hans Dieter Betz, a New Testament scholar, observes, "Prayer, supposedly the most intimate expression of love to God, has turned into its very opposite, preoccupation with oneself." Jesus is saying, when you pray, *God* wants to be the center of your attention.

To counteract our tendency to display our piety before other people, Jesus offers a practical remedy: "Whenever you pray, go into your room and shut the door" (6:6). Throughout chapter 6, in the Greek text, "you" and "your" are plural—except here in verse 6, where "you" and "your" are singular. Go off and pray by *yourself*, Jesus is saying. Go and be alone with God. This point is reinforced by the particular Greek word for "room" here. The word generally refers to rooms in the interior of a house—the innermost room, the back room, the storeroom. In poorer houses, such a room might be the only one with a door. In many cases, it would be windowless and dark. Clearly, Jesus is recommending a place of privacy for our individual prayer.

God is holy, other, hidden from human sight. Often he seems hard to detect in world events and even in the circumstances of our lives. Yet, Jesus assures us, God makes himself known in the place where we might least expect it—in secret, even in darkness. There, in private, God makes himself present to us. We can talk with him and get to know him. German theologian Romano Guardini points out that Jesus does not say,

"If you want to call upon God, go to such-and-such a place, and there you will find Him," or, "Wait for a certain time, and then you may invoke Him," or, "You must do it in such-and-such a way to succeed in making contact." Nothing of the kind! On the contrary, . . . "Simply address yourself to Him who is in Heaven, and your prayer will reach Him." . . . When we stop to consider it, there is something immeasurably marvelous in the fact that God is accessible from anywhere, at any time.

Jesus goes on to criticize long prayers (6:7–8). Unlike the hypocrite, the person who makes wordy appeals may be earnestly focusing on God, seeking rewards that only God can give. Yet the person's picture of God is flawed. Rather than recognize God as a loving Father who knows our needs and has our best interests at heart, the verbose person treats God as an uncaring deity who has to be nagged into paying attention and giving us what we need. The problem that Jesus is addressing lies not in the "many words" (6:7) in and of themselves but in our thinking that many words are necessary to get God to help us.

Long, repetitious prayers may also reflect the mistaken idea that we can get God to do what we want by using the right formulas. In Jesus' day, some non-Jews addressed God with prayers containing many titles, almost like incantations. Having the correct divine titles and repeating them over and over was thought to increase the prayers' effectiveness. But the notion that one can, in effect, turn God into an obedient servant by using the right titles and the proven formulas is closer to magic than to prayer.

Against the picture of God as someone who needs to be shouted at or manipulated, Jesus presents the picture of God as a Father who loves us, knows our real needs (6:8), and does not have to be talked into acting on our behalf.

We might ask, If God already knows what we need, why pray? St. John Chrysostom posed this question in his explanation of the Our Father. His answer: we pray "not to inform God or instruct him but to beseech him closely, to be made intimate with him, by continuance in supplication; to be humbled; to be reminded of our sins."

Fasting: 6:16–18. Finally, Jesus speaks about fasting. Fasting is an act of limiting ourselves, of refusing to satisfy our own desires (for example, our desires to eat or drink) in order to turn to God and become responsive to his desires.

Jesus is critical of those who "disfigure their faces" when they fast (6:16). The meaning of the Greek here is unclear. Were those who fasted not washing their faces as they normally would? Or were they smearing ashes on their faces to draw attention to their fasting? It is impossible to be sure. Jesus also says that when we fast we should wash our faces and put oil on our heads (6:17). But since scholars disagree about whether people in first-century Palestine bathed frequently and routinely used fragrant olive oil, they are uncertain whether Jesus is telling us that when we fast we should make *special* efforts to look happy or should simply go on with our lives as usual.

In any case, the basic point is clear. Fasting is a way of turning to God, of expressing our desire for him and for his action in our lives. If, instead, fasting becomes a way of showing off to other people, the whole exercise is a waste of time. Really, Jesus indicates, it is worse than a waste of time; it is an insult to God. Please, don't bother.

Before we leave this section, a final question is worth considering. Jesus speaks of "hypocrites" in "the synagogues" (6:2, 5). Does he regard Jews as particularly susceptible to the temptation of hypocrisy? Not at all. Jesus is speaking to his fellow Jews about Jews. He is not comparing Jews to other people. He is not saying that hypocrisy is more prevalent among Jews than among gentiles. He does not suggest that the synagogue is a center of hypocrisy. Hypocrisy happens anywhere, he says, on the street as much as in the synagogue (6:2, 5). He does not level his criticism of hypocrisy against the synagogue itself but against those who abuse the synagogue by making it a theater for their own piety. Jesus believes that the synagogue, where Jews customarily studied Scripture and prayed, ought to be a place for paying attention to God. Any good Jew would have agreed with him. Far from condemning the synagogue, Jesus demonstrated a concern for it; he wanted the synagogue to be what it ought to be.

Try substituting the word *church* for *synagogue* in 6:2–5. You will find that Jesus' criticism of hypocrisy works just as well for Christians as for Jews. In any case, Scripture is not given to us as an opportunity for standing in judgment over other people but for discovering and correcting our own failings (see Matthew 7:1–5).

HEAVENLY FATHER!

Questions to Begin

10 minutes
Use a question or two to get warmed up for the reading.

1 When and how did you learn the Lord's Prayer?

2 What other prayers did you learn as a child?

Opening the Bible

10 minutes
Read the passage aloud. Let individuals take turns reading
paragraphs.

The Focus

"Our Father, who art in heaven . . ."

The Reading: Matthew 6:1–18; 7:7–11

Don't Lose Out on Your Reward

6:1 "Beware of practicing your piety before others in order to be seen
by them; for then you have no reward from your Father in heaven."

Practice Kindness Secretly

2 "So whenever you give alms, do not sound a trumpet before you,
as the hypocrites do in the synagogues and in the streets, so that they
may be praised by others. Truly I tell you, they have received their
reward. 3 But when you give alms, do not let your left hand know
what your right hand is doing, 4 so that your alms may be done in
secret; and your Father who sees in secret will reward you."

Keep Your Devotions Private, Too

5 "And whenever you pray, do not be like the hypocrites; for they
love to stand and pray in the synagogues and at the street corners, so
that they may be seen by others. Truly I tell you, they have received
their reward. 6 But whenever you pray, go into your room and shut
the door and pray to your Father who is in secret; and your Father
who sees in secret will reward you.

7 "When you are praying, do not heap up empty phrases as the
Gentiles do; for they think that they will be heard because of their
many words. 8 Do not be like them, for your Father knows what you
need before you ask him.

9 "Pray then in this way:
 Our Father in heaven,
  hallowed be your name.
10 Your kingdom come.
  Your will be done,
   on earth as it is in heaven.
11 Give us this day our daily bread.

¹² 　And forgive us our debts,
　　　　as we also have forgiven our debtors.
¹³ 　And do not bring us to the time of trial,
　　　　but rescue us from the evil one.

¹⁴ "For if you forgive others their trespasses, your heavenly Father will also forgive you; ¹⁵ but if you do not forgive others, neither will your Father forgive your trespasses."

Don't Put Your Piety on Parade

¹⁶ "And whenever you fast, do not look dismal, like the hypocrites, for they disfigure their faces so as to show others that they are fasting. Truly I tell you, they have received their reward. ¹⁷ But when you fast, put oil on your head and wash your face, ¹⁸ so that your fasting may be seen not by others but by your Father who is in secret; and your Father who sees in secret will reward you."

Ask God with Confidence

^{7:7} "Ask, and it will be given you; search, and you will find; knock, and the door will be opened for you. ⁸ For everyone who asks receives, and everyone who searches finds, and for everyone who knocks, the door will be opened. ⁹ Is there anyone among you who, if your child asks for bread, will give a stone? ¹⁰ Or if the child asks for a fish, will give a snake? ¹¹ If you then, who are evil, know how to give good gifts to your children, how much more will your Father in heaven give good things to those who ask him!"

First Impression

5 minutes
Briefly mention a question you have about the reading or one thing in it that surprised, impressed, delighted, or challenged you. No discussion! Just listen to one another's reactions.

*If participants have not read this section already, read it aloud.
Otherwise go on to "Questions for Reflection and Discussion."*

The context (6:1–8, 14–18). After mentioning some basic attitudes for our relationship with God (6:1–8), Jesus introduces his model prayer with an assurance that God knows all about our needs and wants to reward our efforts to turn to him. "Pray then in this way," Jesus says (6:9). In other words, let your prayer be shaped by confidence that God has your best interests at heart. As you begin, consider his love for you.

"Our Father . . ." With these two simple words, we say a great deal about God and about ourselves. Of God, we affirm that he is one, not many, and that he is a person—someone with whom we can have a conversation. Of ourselves, St. Jerome noted, "When we pray 'Father,' we acknowledge that we ourselves are his children." Thus, with the first words of the prayer, we affirm that we did not tumble into the world by chance; we are here because a Father has willed us into existence. Our lives have a purpose, which, even if it is hidden from us, is known by the one to whom we are beginning to speak.

Calling God *Father* strikes a note of familiarity. For myself, I can say that this familiarity becomes more and more astonishing as I realize more and more clearly how little I understand of the immense universe in which we live. Yet I, who cannot understand the created universe, can experience the creator being close to me. Like my father when I was a little boy, God bends down to listen when I speak to him. Amazing!

Acknowledging God as sole creator and ruler of all is fundamental in Judaism. Jews know that God is merciful and faithful, a loving guide and teacher. In Jesus' day, however, Jews did not think of God mainly as *Father*. Only rarely did they address him that way. But for Jesus, God is *essentially* Father. Jesus often spoke of God as Father (in this week's reading, see 6:1, 4, 6, 8, 14, 18; 7:11) and addressed God this way in his own prayer (more on this in Week 5). Jesus experienced God as an affectionate Father and, Jesus revealed, this is how God is toward us, too. In a sense, the whole purpose of Jesus' mission in the world is to share with us his own Son-to-Father relationship with God. To pray the first words of the Lord's Prayer is to accept this offer of an intimate relationship with God.

St. Thomas Aquinas tells us that "of all the things required of us when we pray, confidence is of great avail. For this reason, our Lord, in teaching us how to pray, mentions those things which instill confidence in us, such as the loving kindness of a father implied in the words, *Our Father.*" With these opening words, we open our hearts to God as little children (see Matthew 19:14). At the same time, these opening words imply an adult commitment to behave as God's children, to obey him, and to accept the responsibility of imitating him (see 5:48).

Before moving on, it is worth giving a little thought also to the very first word of the prayer: "our." When we say "our," who is the "we" that we have in mind? Does it include only those who are close to us? Is the "we"—asked Ukrainian archbishop Andrey Sheptytsky—only those who belong to our ethnic group, our nation? Isn't it, he replied, "all of us who have been redeemed by Christ's Blood? Does it even include the unbaptized? Does it relate to those who live, or also those who have not yet been born, or even those who died long ago?" The word *our* is very small, the archbishop observed. "But what boundless prospects it presents, how it expands the heart and soul to yet unknown limits. The feeling of human solidarity knows no bounds, nor does it know the limitation of a heart which, satisfied with what it possesses, is unwilling to share with others." Thus, when we call on God as "our" Father, we include in the "we" all who call him Father and, indeed, all whom God considers to be his children, regardless of what they think of him. And we accept the obligation of treating them as our brothers and sisters.

"Who art in heaven . . ." What do these words add? Surely we already know where God is. The point, however, is not to identify God's location but to distinguish him from every other source of life. With these words we make a distinction between our heavenly Parent and our earthly mothers and fathers. We affirm that the gift of life that came to us through our parents originated in our heavenly Father. He is the source of our lives.

The words "who art in heaven" also remind us that while God is intimate and affectionate with us like a father, he remains far above us, unseen, beyond our comprehension. Romano Guardini wrote that "heaven" here signifies "the inaccessibility of God." Heaven, Guardini said,

is that blessed, inviolable freedom in which He belongs to Himself, as He who is. . . . *Heaven* stands for the otherness of God. . . . We must raise our minds from the earth when we address God, who is in Heaven. . . . We must admit that He is not like things or like time or like ourselves. We do not prescribe to Him what He is to be like, but are agreed that He is the One who is of Himself. . . . And we are prepared for the fact that He is different from our expectations, mysterious and unknown. . . . The words "in Heaven" say, "I want You, God, as You are in Yourself." And in uttering them, the Christian takes the risk, as it were, of having this God come into his life; of having the everyday tenor of his own life disturbed by the entry of God, the Other, the Inscrutable.

Further on in his sermon, Jesus adds a remark about praying to God as our Father (7:7–11). Because God *is* our Father, he says, we should keep on praying to him when we do not receive what we ask for.

Does this instruction conflict with Jesus' earlier prohibition against long prayers (6:7–8)? Not really. The two instructions have a common root: relating to God as a real father. Using lengthy prayers as though they were magical formulas disregards God's fatherly love. Likewise, we disregard his fatherly love if we stop talking to him when we do not immediately receive what we ask for.

Our heavenly Father will give us "good things," Jesus assures us (7:11). This does not mean he will give us whatever we ask. God knows what is good for us; often we do not. Our first parents, as depicted in the Bible, acted as though they knew better than God what was good for them (Genesis 3). Jesus urges us, instead, to trust God's wisdom and ask him for what *he* considers good for us. What is that? The rest of the prayer will provide excellent guidance.

Questions for Reflection and Discussion

45 minutes
Choose questions according to your interest and time.

1 Why would a person want to have his or her religious practices be "seen" (6:5) and "praised" (6:2) by other people?

2 Reread 6:3. Jesus sometimes exaggerated to make a point (see also 5:29–30). What is the value of this kind of exaggeration? What are the dangers?

3 Reread 6:7. What picture of God is in the mind of the person who prays like this? How is this different from the picture of God that Jesus reveals?

4 How can a person do good in a way that points people's attention not to himself or herself but to God?

5 Who has been an example to you of helping others without calling attention to themselves?

6 Jesus urges us to please God rather than enhance our reputation (6:1–6, 16–17), to speak to God simply and directly (6:7–8), to have confidence that God knows all about us and wants to reward our efforts (6:6–8). In what ways does the Our Father meet these criteria for prayer?

7 How might a person's experiences of their father and mother have a positive or negative effect on their relationship with God? How does God show himself to be more loving than any human parent?

8 Jesus repeatedly says that "your Father who sees in secret will reward you" (6:4, 6, 18). What benefits do you seek when you pray? Do you receive them?

9 **Focus question.** What has helped you experience God as your Father? How has God shown himself to be your Father? How has this affected your relationship with him?

Prayer to Close

10 minutes
Use this approach—or create your own!

♦ Let someone read Romans 8:14–17 aloud. Pause for a minute of silent reflection. Then pray "Our Father, who art in heaven" together and pause, giving one person the opportunity to express a short prayer; for example, "Help my son to find a job" or "Guide our leaders to the road to peace," and so on. Pray "Our Father, who art in heaven" again, letting another person offer a prayer. Continue in the same way until everyone who wishes to pray has had a chance to do so. Conclude by praying the whole Our Father together.

Saints in the Making

Surprised by His Father

This section is a supplement for individual reading.

By Fio Mascerenhas, SJ

In 1968, for the first time, I failed a university examination. I had joined the Society of Jesus in 1963, after graduating in chemistry. My superior sent me back to the university to specialize so that I could become a professor of chemistry in our Jesuit university in Bombay. I was very happy. I said to myself, "I'm going to be a famous professor of chemistry." In my daydreams I even dreamed that one day I would get the Nobel Prize for chemistry.

So you can imagine my consternation, shock, confusion, and humiliation when I failed the exam. This was something quite extraordinary, because I knew everything and I had gotten the gold medal at the university the previous year. Everybody was expecting me to top the class. But as I walked into the examination hall, my mind went blank. I couldn't remember anything.

I appeared for the exam a second time some months later, again preparing myself very well. But again, as I walked into the examination hall, my mind went blank. And I failed the second time.

I appeared for that examination a third time. This time, as I walked into the hall, I whispered this prayer: "I know, Lord, that you don't love me. So I'm not going to ask you anything for myself. But I hope you still love my poor mother." Mummy had been making novena after novena and offering Masses that her poor Fio would pass the exam. But my mind went blank there in the hall. And I failed the third time.

This was a real crisis of faith. I stopped praying to God. I could not believe that God loved me. When people said, "Pray more," I said, "That's all rubbish." And slowly I began to rebel within myself. I became bitter, turned in upon myself.

Spiritually, I could not believe in God, and I was rebellious. Emotionally, I could not face people anymore; I thought they would be laughing at me because of my three failures. Physically, I had suffered from asthma all my life, and in these days I was hospitalized many times. I could not walk much. I was gasping for breath most of the time. I had all kinds of dietary restrictions.

One day I was moved to kneel before my crucifix. As I knelt before that crucifix I could sense a prayer coming from deep within.

I felt myself saying, "Lord, I am useless. I have no future. But if you have a plan for my life, here I am." All along before that, I was telling the Lord what he had to do for me. Now I was saying, "Lord, if you have a plan for me, here I am."

Immediately, even as I was kneeling there, the response of God became clear to me. It was a voice that spoke to me interiorly, "Fio, you are my beloved son in whom I am well pleased." At once, my mind started working. "Well pleased? How can he be well pleased with me?" And yet, though I could not understand it intellectually, from deep within my heart a joy began to bubble up. I leapt to my feet, threw my hands up in the air, and shouted, "Jesus, you're alive!"

That was my baptism in the Holy Spirit. I was completely healed in three ways. Physically, I was healed. Since then I've never had a problem with asthma. I told you I had dietary problems. Until then, I couldn't eat ice cream. Now I can. A whole bucket if you give it to me!

Emotionally, I was healed. I told you I could not face people. But God's saying to me, "Fio, you are my beloved son," gave me a new sense of my own self-worth, not based on human achievement, but on the realization that God loves me; I am his son.

Spiritually, I was healed. I now have an intuitive, spontaneous conviction that God loves me. That brings up within me a deep sense of humility and a sense of tremendous gratitude to God.

So what happened to my chemistry? I appeared for that examination a fourth time—soon after this experience of baptism in the Holy Spirit—and everything went well. I passed with a first class. As a result, I'm qualified to teach chemistry at any university in the world. But do you know, I never taught chemistry again!

When I was ordained in 1975, three years after my baptism in the Spirit, my Jesuit provincial said: "Fio, you are qualified for two apostolates. Which do you want to choose?" I said, "What are they?" He said, "Well, of course, there's chemistry. But you had an experience of God, and you are able to communicate it to others. Why don't you get into the charismatic renewal and be full-time for it?"

Over the years I have had the opportunity to go to over eighty countries to speak at conferences. Wherever I went, I would ask people, "If I was a chemistry professor, would you have invited me here?" From this I realized that God did the best thing he could do for me by bringing me through that period of suffering. Otherwise I probably would have been too proud and too much a "head" person to get involved in the charismatic renewal.

To God, each one of us is a son or a daughter first—a sinner second. That was my experience. I was a sinner. I rebelled against God. I had given up prayer. I did not believe in him anymore. And yet, he loved me first. It is not because I deserved it, but because he knew that I was misguided, lost in the desert. His amazing grace came to bring sight to my eyes and to bring hope into my life.

Look at the parable of the prodigal son. Here was a boy who had rebelled—who in every way was a sinner. As he came back to his father he recognized, "I can never be a son again. I will always be a sinner." And what did he do? He came to his father thinking he would say: "I am no longer worthy to be your son. Treat me as a servant." But the father would have nothing to do with that attitude. He ran and he embraced his boy and said: "You are my son first and always. Nothing can change this, not even your sins." In grace and in disgrace, we remain sons and daughters.

So, when Jesus taught us to pray, he said, "First remember that you are a child and cry out as a child, 'Abba! Dear Daddy! Our Father!'"

YOUR NAME, YOUR REIGN, YOUR WILL

Questions to Begin

10 minutes
Use a question or two to get warmed up for the reading.

1 Why did your parents give you the name, or names, they gave you?

2 Have you ever had any reason to be especially happy or unhappy about your given name? about your surname?

Opening the Bible

10 minutes
Read the passage aloud. Let individuals take turns reading paragraphs.

The Focus

". . . hallowed be thy name; thy kingdom come; thy will be done on earth as it is in heaven . . ."

The Background

Early in his Gospel, Matthew shows Jesus striking the keynote of his preaching: he announces that God's kingdom is at hand (4:17, 23). The coming of God's kingdom is the focus of Jesus' ministry—of his teaching and healing and also of his ultimate self-sacrifice on the cross. In his model prayer, Jesus urges us to join him in focusing our attention on the coming of God's kingdom. Further on in the Sermon on the Mount (6:19–33), he calls us to make the coming of this kingdom the center of our lives.

The Reading: Matthew 4:17, 23; 6:9–13, 19–21, 24–33

God's Kingdom Is Near!

4:17 From that time Jesus began to proclaim, "Repent, for the kingdom of heaven has come near." . . . 23 Jesus went throughout Galilee, teaching in their synagogues and proclaiming the good news of the kingdom and curing every disease and every sickness among the people.

Pray for the Coming of the Kingdom

6:9 "Pray then in this way:
    Our Father in heaven,
        hallowed be your name.
10   Your kingdom come.
    Your will be done,
        on earth as it is in heaven.
11   Give us this day our daily bread.
12   And forgive us our debts,
        as we also have forgiven our debtors.

13   And do not bring us to the time of trial,
          but rescue us from the evil one."

Make the Kingdom Your Highest Priority

19 "Do not store up for yourselves treasures on earth, where moth and rust consume and where thieves break in and steal; 20 but store up for yourselves treasures in heaven, where neither moth nor rust consumes and where thieves do not break in and steal. 21 For where your treasure is, there your heart will be also. . . .

24 "No one can serve two masters; for a slave will either hate the one and love the other, or be devoted to the one and despise the other. You cannot serve God and wealth.

25 "Therefore I tell you, do not worry about your life, what you will eat or what you will drink, or about your body, what you will wear. Is not life more than food, and the body more than clothing? 26 Look at the birds of the air; they neither sow nor reap nor gather into barns, and yet your heavenly Father feeds them. Are you not of more value than they? 27 And can any of you by worrying add a single hour to your span of life? 28 And why do you worry about clothing? Consider the lilies of the field, how they grow; they neither toil nor spin, 29 yet I tell you, even Solomon in all his glory was not clothed like one of these. 30 But if God so clothes the grass of the field, which is alive today and tomorrow is thrown into the oven, will he not much more clothe you—you of little faith?

31 "Therefore do not worry, saying, 'What will we eat?' or 'What will we drink?' or 'What will we wear?' 32 For it is the Gentiles who strive for all these things; and indeed your heavenly Father knows that you need all these things. 33 But strive first for the kingdom of God and his righteousness, and all these things will be given to you as well."

First Impression

5 minutes
Briefly mention a question you have about the reading or one thing in it that surprised, impressed, delighted, or challenged you. No discussion! Just listen to one another's reactions.

Exploring the Theme

If participants have not read this section already, read it aloud.
Otherwise go on to "Questions for Reflection and Discussion."

The Lord's Prayer is the most perfect of prayers, St. Thomas Aquinas declared, because in it we not only ask for all the things we can rightly desire but we also ask for them in the sequence in which they should be desired. By guiding us to start our prayer by focusing on *God's* name, *God's* kingdom, and *God's* will, Jesus teaches us, quite simply, to put our own concerns on hold and to pay attention to God. In a sense, this is the natural reaction of anyone who, at the beginning of prayer, looks up to God and feels awe at God's greatness and goodness.

"Hallowed be thy name . . ." What is the meaning of "name" here? The authors of Scripture sometimes treat God's "name" as though the word itself were a kind of sacrament of his presence. The *name* of God was similar, in a way, to the temple in Jerusalem, which was a *place* where God made himself especially present. Sometimes, God's "name" was a way of referring to God himself (Deuteronomy 12:11; 14:23). Thus, for example, God said, "I have chosen Jerusalem in order that my name may be there"—by which he meant that he himself would be present there (2 Chronicles 6:6). In a similar way, in the Our Father, "name" refers to God himself. We are saying to God, "May *you* be hallowed." But what does it mean to *hallow*?

To *hallow* is to "make holy." Now, the one who is primarily holy is God. His holiness is his grandeur, his power—his *otherness* from all else that is. In one sense, only God is holy. Yet he is also the source of holiness for others. He makes persons and things holy by removing them from ordinary use and setting them aside for his service. Thus, to *make holy,* or hallow, or sanctify, means to make someone or something the possession of God in a special way (Exodus 31:13; Leviticus 21:8, 15, 23; Ezekiel 20:12). God, then, is the one who *hallows*.

Yet the Hebrew word for *hallow* may also mean "to recognize as holy," to sanctify God in the sense of acknowledging him as the source of holiness (Isaiah 29:23). In this sense, hallowing is something that creatures do. In a vision, the prophet Isaiah saw God enthroned in heaven, flanked by mysterious winged guardians called seraphs. As the seraphs hovered beside God, they cried out to each other, "Holy, holy, holy is the Lord of hosts; the whole earth is full of his glory" (Isaiah 6:1–3). The seraphs beheld God's splendor and responded with wonder, awe, appreciation, and delight. They recognized God's holiness and proclaimed it to each other. This is a classic example of *hallowing* God's name. It is a clue to what we are asking for in the Lord's Prayer. In effect we are saying to God, "May we and everyone else acknowledge your holiness and relate to you as the Holy One! Like the seraphs, may all people give you glory, praise you, love you, and serve you."

In order to hallow God, of course, people need to have their eyes opened to his holiness. So this is implied in our request. We are asking God to let his splendor shine out, so that everyone will be filled with amazement, gratitude, and respect for him. God promised the prophet Ezekiel, "I will display my greatness and my holiness and make myself known in the eyes of many nations. Then they shall know that I am the Lord" (Ezekiel 38:23). In a sense, in the Lord's Prayer, we respond to this promise. "Yes, indeed, Father," we say. "Do just that!"

In essence, God shows his holiness and draws people to acclaim him by revealing his love (Psalms 111:9; 115:1–2; Ezekiel 20:41–42; 28:25; 36:23; 38:16; 39:27; John 12:28). Scripture speaks of this process as God *showing his glory.* God's glory is both his greatness and magnificence and also his mercy and love (Exodus 16:6–7—God will show his glory by feeding the Israelites; 33:18–34:7; John 17). God shows his glory, and people glorify him in return when he gives them an experience of both his power and majesty and of his compassion and kindness.

We pray this first petition sincerely only if we are willing to let God's glory become visible in us. God created us in his image (Genesis 1:26–27) so that we might reflect his goodness. Thus, Jesus urges us: "Let your light shine before others, so that they may see your good works and give glory to your Father in heaven" (Matthew 5:16). If we really want God's name to be hallowed, we will give our fellow human beings a taste of his love.

"Thy kingdom come . . ." In one sense, God's kingdom is a place we enter (Matthew 7:21). In another sense, God's kingdom is a reign, an exercise of dominion, to which we submit ourselves (Matthew 3:2; 4:17).

Doesn't God already reign over everything? Of course, he does, St. Augustine writes. But "just as light that is present is absent to the blind or to those who shut their eyes, so the reign of God, though it never departs from the earth, is absent to those who know nothing about it." So we pray that God's reign would be known and experienced by all.

St. Thomas Aquinas wrote that God's kingdom here signifies the glory of paradise. "Since God wills men to be saved, the will of God will be realized most especially in paradise, where there will be nothing contrary to man's salvation. When, therefore, we pray *Thy kingdom come*, we ask to be made partakers of the heavenly kingdom and of the glory of paradise."

In one sense, God's kingdom is a *future* reality, toward which we are moving throughout history. In praying for God's kingdom, we are praying for God to complete his work with the human race. Yet God's kingdom is also *present*. It began to arrive in Jesus' teaching and healing, and especially in his death and resurrection. God's kingdom is already accessible by faith in Jesus. With the help of the Holy Spirit, we can experience it, in a hidden way, here and now (Romans 14:17–18). Thus it is also for a deeper, present experience of God's kingdom that we pray in the Our Father. We pray, St. Augustine wrote, that the kingdom would come upon us and that we would be humble enough not to resist it.

In its explanation of the Our Father, the old Catholic *Catechism* (of 1566) quoted St. Paul's statement "It is no longer I who live, but it is Christ who lives in me" (Galatians 2:20). "Accordingly," the catechism observed, "we may also say, 'I reign, yet not I, but Christ reigns in me.' . . . We pray that God alone may live and reign within us so that death at last will no longer exist. . . . We pray that, having broken and scattered the power of his enemies, Jesus Christ may by his mighty power subject all things to his dominion (see 1 Corinthians 15:23–24)."

This hope, Jesus declares, should be the focus of our lives (Matthew 6:33).

"Thy will be done . . ." By itself, this petition might sound like a fatalistic sigh of resignation to whatever misfortune may befall us. In context, however, it is an appeal for God to act. We have just prayed for God to show his holiness and extend his reign. Now we ask him to accomplish his purposes.

What purposes? "God wills," St. Thomas answers, "that man be restored to the state and dignity in which the first man was created, which was so great that his spirit and soul experienced no rebellion on the part of his flesh and sensuality." In other words, God's will is to recreate us, so that with our whole being we would love him, without any inner temptation to turn away from him. Of course, Thomas observes, this will of God cannot be completed in this life. But it will be fulfilled at the resurrection, when Christ returns.

Since God's will is our complete transformation, this is something that only he can do. Yet, again, by asking him for it, we are also expressing a willingness to do our part. And, in light of the fact that our part in the accomplishment of God's will is sometimes arduous, we are implicitly asking for his help. St. Teresa of Ávila said to Jesus: "Since my earth has now become Heaven"—Teresa meant, "since you have come to live within me"—"it will be possible for Thy will to be done in me. Otherwise, on an earth so wretched as mine, and so barren of fruit, I know not, Lord, how it could be possible." Because it is sometimes hard to obey God, Teresa warned her sisters in the convent not to suppose they could reach the state of total obedience to God's will by their own efforts or diligence. "That would be too much to expect. On the contrary, you would turn what devotion you had quite cold. You must practice simplicity and humility, for those are the virtues which achieve everything." We must rely on God's help in order to do his will.

"On earth as it is in heaven . . ." By this phrase, Jesus indicates the degree to which we should wish to see God praised, loved, and obeyed. As the angels serve God faultlessly in heaven, St. Jerome explained, so may human beings serve him on earth.

Questions for Reflection and Discussion

45 minutes
Choose questions according to your interest and time.

1 Reread 4:23. In what way did Jesus' proclamation that God's kingdom is near show the meaning of his remarkable activities (his healings, multiplying bread, and so on)? In what way did Jesus' activities show the meaning of his proclamation of God's kingdom?

2 What kinds of riches are attacked by moths and rust (6:19–20)? What kinds of forces erode wealth today?

3 How would you explain what Jesus is saying in 6:21?

4 Reread 6:24. In what ways can wealth be a master? What experience have you had of what Jesus is saying here?

5 When have you had the experience of seeing God's name? What impact has this experience had on you?

6 Jesus tells us to pray for the coming of God's kingdom *and* to strive for it (6:10, 33). What is the relationship between praying and working for God's kingdom in your life?

7 How could you make the coming of God's kingdom a higher priority in your life?

8 For personal reflection: Where in your life is there a struggle of wills between you and God? Reflect on this situation and express your thoughts to God, asking for his help to embrace his will.

9 **Focus question.** What action could you take to contribute to God's name being hallowed? What could you do so that his goodness and love might be recognized by at least one person?

Prayer to Close

10 minutes
Use this approach—or create your own!

♦ Ask someone to read aloud St. Paul's prayer for his fellow Christians in Ephesians 1:17–19. Pause for silent reflection. Ask someone else to read this prayer aloud:

Father, open our eyes to the great power of Christ your Son living in our hearts. Help us to notice where you are at work in our lives and in the world—and help us to cooperate with you.

Allow time for individual members to add brief prayers for various needs. End by praying the Our Father together.

GIVE US OUR BREAD

Questions to Begin

10 minutes
Use a question or two to get warmed up for the reading.

1 What's your favorite kind of bread—or your favorite substitute for bread?

2 Do you ever bake bread? What kind?

Opening the Bible

10 minutes
Read the passage aloud. Let individuals take turns reading
paragraphs.

The Focus

". . . Give us this day our daily bread . . ."

The Background

More than a thousand years before the time of Jesus, God led the
Israelites out of Egypt, where they had been enslaved, and brought
them into Canaan (present-day Israel and Palestine), where they
could live in dignity and freedom. Their journey from Egypt to Canaan
took many years, and along the way they encountered various
problems from neighboring people, from the natural environment,
and from themselves. In our first reading, the Israelites have just
escaped from Egypt and are wandering in the Sinai Peninsula—a
barren wilderness of sand and rock, broiling hot during most of the
year. The little food they brought with them from Egypt has run out.

In our second reading, Jesus delivers a sermon in the
synagogue of Capernaum, the town that serves as his base of
operations during his traveling ministry in Galilee. The day before this
sermon, he miraculously multiplied bread to feed a large crowd. The
people in his audience now would probably like to see another such
miracle. But Jesus directs their attention to a different kind of bread.

The Reading: Exodus 16:2–4, 6–7, 13–16, 19–21, 31, 35; John 6:30–35, 47–58; Matthew 6:9–13

A Daily Miracle in Sinai

Exodus 16:2 The whole congregation of the Israelites complained
against Moses and Aaron in the wilderness. 3 The Israelites said to
them, "If only we had died by the hand of the LORD in the land of
Egypt, when we sat by the fleshpots and ate our fill of bread; for you
have brought us out into this wilderness to kill this whole assembly
with hunger."

4 Then the LORD said to Moses, "I am going to rain bread
from heaven for you, and each day the people shall go out and gather

enough for that day. In that way I will test them, whether they will follow my instruction or not." . . .

6 So Moses and Aaron said to all the Israelites, "In the evening you shall know that it was the LORD who brought you out of the land of Egypt, 7 and in the morning you shall see the glory of the LORD, because he has heard your complaining against the LORD. . . ."

13 . . . In the morning there was a layer of dew around the camp. 14 When the layer of dew lifted, there on the surface of the wilderness was a fine flaky substance, as fine as frost on the ground. 15 When the Israelites saw it, they said to one another, "What is it?" For they did not know what it was. Moses said to them, "It is the bread that the LORD has given you to eat. 16 This is what the LORD has commanded: 'Gather as much of it as each of you needs. . . .'"

19 And Moses said to them, "Let no one leave any of it over until morning." 20 But they did not listen to Moses; some left part of it until morning, and it bred worms and became foul. And Moses was angry with them. 21 Morning by morning they gathered it, as much as each needed; but when the sun grew hot, it melted. . . .

31 The house of Israel called it manna; it was like coriander seed, white, and the taste of it was like wafers made with honey. . . . 35 The Israelites ate manna forty years, until they came to a habitable land; they ate manna, until they came to the border of the land of Canaan.

A Sabbath Sermon in Capernaum

John 6:30 They said to him, . . . 31 "Our ancestors ate the manna in the wilderness; as it is written, 'He gave them bread from heaven to eat.'"

32 Then Jesus said to them, "Very truly, I tell you, it was not Moses who gave you the bread from heaven, but it is my Father who gives you the true bread from heaven. 33 For the bread of God is that which comes down from heaven and gives life to the world."

34 They said to him, "Sir, give us this bread always."

35 Jesus said to them, "I am the bread of life. Whoever comes to me will never be hungry, and whoever believes in me will never be thirsty. . . . 47 Very truly, I tell you, whoever believes has eternal life. 48 I

am the bread of life. [49] Your ancestors ate the manna in the wilderness, and they died. [50] This is the bread that comes down from heaven, so that one may eat of it and not die. [51] I am the living bread that came down from heaven. Whoever eats of this bread will live forever; and the bread that I will give for the life of the world is my flesh."

[52] The Jews then disputed among themselves, saying, "How can this man give us his flesh to eat?"

[53] So Jesus said to them, "Very truly, I tell you, unless you eat the flesh of the Son of Man and drink his blood, you have no life in you. [54] Those who eat my flesh and drink my blood have eternal life, and I will raise them up on the last day; [55] for my flesh is true food and my blood is true drink. [56] Those who eat my flesh and drink my blood abide in me, and I in them. [57] Just as the living Father sent me, and I live because of the Father, so whoever eats me will live because of me. [58] This is the bread that came down from heaven, not like that which your ancestors ate, and they died. But the one who eats this bread will live forever."

The Lord's Prayer

Matthew 6:9 "Pray then in this way:
Our Father in heaven,
hallowed be your name.
[10] Your kingdom come.
Your will be done,
on earth as it is in heaven.
[11] Give us this day our daily bread.
[12] And forgive us our debts,
as we also have forgiven our debtors.
[13] And do not bring us to the time of trial,
but rescue us from the evil one."

First Impression

5 minutes
Briefly mention a question you have about the reading or one thing in it that surprised, impressed, delighted, or challenged you. No discussion! Just listen to one another's reactions.

Exploring the Theme

If participants have not read this section already, read it aloud. Otherwise go on to "Questions for Reflection and Discussion."

The first three petitions of the Lord's Prayer focus our attention on God and his agenda for the human race. In the remaining four petitions, we speak to him about our needs. At the top of our list is a very basic requirement: "bread." But what exactly is this bread for which we pray?

1. The just-bread interpretation. St. John Chrysostom, a fourth-century bishop, understood "bread" here to be simply nourishment for our bodies. We must eat to live, Chrysostom said, and Jesus designed the petition to express this elemental need. (And notice, Chrysostom added, that Jesus guides us to limit our request. We are to ask God not for riches, pleasures, expensive clothing, or anything extravagant but merely for bread, that is, what we actually need.)

But does Jesus mean only the sandwichable kind of bread? In the first three petitions, we look up to heaven and ask God to unfold his plans. In the last three petitions, as we will see, we focus on our cooperation with God's plans, asking him to forgive our failures to cooperate with him in the past and seeking his help for being faithful to him in the future. Since these six petitions are concerned with God's plans being carried out in the world and in our lives, we might expect that the petition for bread, in the middle of the prayer, would share these concerns also. Certainly, we need material nourishment to cooperate with God's plans. Yet it would seem odd if Jesus urged us to seek only the kind of nourishment that sustains our bodies. He sometimes used bread as a pointer to larger realities. For example, after miraculously providing ordinary bread for thousands of people, he told them that they should seek a different kind of bread—the kind that gives eternal life (John 6:26–27). So we may suspect that when he mentions bread in his model prayer, he has more than loaves in mind.

2. The not-just-bread interpretation. A fourth-century deacon, St. Ephrem, held that the petition for bread does not concern material bread at all. He wrote:

It is unnecessary to ask the divine giver of all good things for anything except his reign and his justice, for everything else will be generously granted to us (Matthew 6:33), even if we do not ask for it. We insult God's infinite power and mercy if we ask him for anything besides the glory of his kingdom. . . . Let us, then, ask for a table filled with heavenly food; then our daily bread will increase. Let us desire immortal goods, and we will not lack for the mortal ones.

Thus, St. Ephrem offered this paraphrase of the fourth petition: "Supply for our weakness, without our asking, this bread that we have in common with the animals. But fulfill our prayers by granting us your kingdom, which is worthy of your majesty and your generosity."

But maybe St. Ephrem swung the pendulum a little too far in the opposite direction. Jesus instructed us not to worry about our earthly needs, but he never told us not to *pray* for them. God holds our lives in his hands and knows our needs better than we do (6:8), Jesus assures us, so we should have no anxiety about them. But the way to overcome our anxiety and trust in God's care is to keep talking with God about our needs.

3. Combining the two interpretations. It seems that the best interpretation of "bread" in the Lord's Prayer would combine St. John Chrysostom's and St. Ephrem's insights. We humans have both a physical and a spiritual dimension. Thus, we need both material and spiritual nourishment. To live and fulfill God's purposes, we need bread on the table and also, as St. Ephrem put it, "heavenly food." Can we be more specific about what this spiritual bread might be?

4. Spiritual meanings of bread. On one occasion, the Devil tempted Jesus to change stones into loaves of bread. In reply, Jesus quoted Scripture: a human being "does not live by bread alone, but by every word that comes from the mouth of God" (Matthew 4:4, quoting Deuteronomy 8:3). Thus, Jesus spoke of God's word as a kind of bread—indeed, as bread more important than ordinary bread (see also John 4:32–34). By God's word, he meant God's commandments, wisdom, guidance, and so on. This spiritual bread of God's word, Jesus asserted, is crucial for human life.

Jesus also spoke of himself as bread—"the true bread" (John 6:32). He was referring to the Eucharist. In the Eucharist, Jesus makes himself bread for our nourishment by transforming bread into himself. In this way, he enters into us and becomes our source of eternal life inside us. Thus, Tertullian, a second-century Christian teacher, explained that the petition for bread in the Our Father refers to Christ, since "Christ is our bread." Citing Jesus' declaration in the synagogue at Capernaum, "I am the bread of life" (John 6:35), and his declaration regarding the bread at the Last Supper, "This is my body" (Matthew 26:26), Tertullian concluded, "When we ask for our daily bread, we are asking that we should perpetually be in Christ and that we should not be separated from his body."

Bringing together the material and spiritual interpretations, St. Augustine wrote that in the Our Father, "we ask for our daily bread, which is necessary for our body, and also for the visible sacrament of the Word of God," by which he meant the Eucharist, "and for the invisible sacrament," by which he meant the word of God, especially in Scripture and in the liturgy.

Teresa of Ávila believed that Jesus deliberately left "bread" in the petition open to many interpretations so as to embrace the wide range of human needs. "This prayer was meant to be a general one for the use of all, so that everyone could interpret it as he thought right, ask for what he wanted and find comfort in doing so." Thus, she said, contemplatives in a monastery can ask for · "heavenly favours" while those who have families and jobs can ask for everything "they need for their own maintenance and for that of their households, as is perfectly just and right, and they may also ask for other things according as they need them."

The petition seems to have a further dimension. In the request for bread, we may hear an echo of the manna, the mysterious food that God gave the Israelites on their forty-year journey from Egypt to Canaan. There are, in fact, several similarities between the manna and the bread of the Lord's Prayer. Like the "bread" of the prayer, the manna was sometimes simply called "bread" (Exodus 16:8, 12, 15). The emphasis on "today" in the Lord's Prayer ("give us *this day* our daily bread") recalls the daily quality of the manna: each day's manna lasted only for that day, forcing the Israelites to gather up fresh manna each morning. In addition, "heaven" is mentioned in the Our Father just before the request for bread, while the manna was often called "bread from heaven" (Exodus 16:4; Nehemiah 9:15; see also Wisdom 16:20; Psalm 78:23–25; 1 Corinthians 10:3). So it seems that in his prayer Jesus is alluding to the manna of the Israelites' wilderness journey.

Such an allusion enhances the meaning of the petition. First, the Israelites ate the manna while they traveled to the land God had in store for them. The manna was food for a journey. If we now ask God for our manna in the Our Father, we remind ourselves that we, too, are travelers during our earthly life, moving toward God's kingdom. Thus, we do not ask him for bread—the nourishment and resources—for building a permanent home in the present world, but rather for his help in making our way along each day's segment of the trip. Second, the manna was God's sustenance for people who were in a desperate situation. In the barren Sinai Peninsula, the Israelites faced starvation. Through the manna, God miraculously sustained them. Asking for our manna today, we express our trust that God is able to sustain us even in the most difficult circumstances.

In his sermon in the Capernaum synagogue, Jesus likened himself to the manna. In fact, he declared that he *is* the true manna for our earthly journey to God's kingdom. Unlike the manna that the Israelites received, Jesus does not pass away each day. He is the ever-living source of eternal life (John 6:50–51, 54, 58). Yet we need him anew each day. We cannot assimilate all of God's Word, all of Christ's life, in a day, or even in a lifetime. So we pray for our manna every day, until we reach our eternal home in God.

Questions for Reflection and Discussion

45 minutes
Choose questions according to your interest and time.

1 Reread Exodus 16:2–3. Did the Israelites ask God to sustain them in the wilderness? Did they pray for their daily bread? What do their words indicate about their attitude toward God?

2 Each day's manna lasted only for a day (Exodus 16:20–21), so the Israelites had to go out to gather fresh manna every morning. What might have been God's purpose for sending the manna this way?

3 When have you been especially conscious that God was providing what you needed? How does that provision inspire you to live today?

4 What bread—nourishment, resource—do you most need in order to do God's will at this present time in your life? Have you been asking God for what you need? Do you believe that he will provide it?

5 What one thing could you do this week to help someone get the bread they need?

6 Is reading and praying Scripture part of your daily nourishment? What could you do to improve this part of your diet?

7 How have you experienced Jesus in the Eucharist as the bread of your life? How could you open yourself to be nourished more deeply by him?

8 **Focus question.** How does seeing life as a journey to God's kingdom affect the way a person makes decisions? Who have you known that viewed his or her life as a journey toward God? What could you learn from that person?

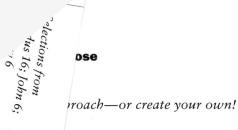

roach—or create your own!

♦ Ask someone to pray this prayer
by Blessed John XXIII aloud.
Allow time for participants to
express brief prayers. End with
an Our Father.

O living Bread,
who came down from heaven to
    give life to the world!
O loving Shepherd of souls, a
    hidden God,
who pour out your grace
on families and peoples,
we commend to you
particularly those who are sick,
    unhappy, poor,
and all who beg for food and
    employment,
imploring for all and everyone
    the assistance of your
    providence;
we commend to you the families
so that they may be fruitful
    centers of Christian life.
May the abundance of your
    grace be poured over all.

Saints in the Making

Trusting the Father

This section is a supplement for individual reading.

By Marie Céres Marcelus

I have many, many miracles in my life!

I always ask God, "Give me life to raise my children and educate them. Give me more courage, and make me stronger. Give me more faith so that I can be spiritually full."

Very often, when I ask God for something, I get it by faith. I prayed to get married, and God arranged it. Twice when I was pregnant, the doctor said I needed a C-section. I didn't want to, because of the recovery time, and because I didn't have any money. I prayed and said, "God, I know you are more powerful than the doctor. If the doctor can operate on me, you can operate on me, too." And those two births were normal.

I ask God for spiritual food first, and after that he will give me what I need materially. I know that man does not live by bread alone but by the words of God. I teach my children this, even when they're small. I always teach them to pray, because God is first in your life.

I pray because I know God is my Lord. I say, "You are my master. Take my life. Direct me, and put me any place you want. If you teach me, I will learn." I know that life will be tough for me otherwise, if I take my own direction.

My husband isn't working, and neither am I. Two of my children are in school; two don't go, because I can't afford to send them. I haven't found work for five years, but I always get something to eat and feed my kids and my husband. When I have a need and don't know what to do, I say to God, "I know you are bigger than my need. I don't have any food to give my children today, but I know you are the one who gives me bread before I even ask you, and so I am going to ask for the spiritual bread first, because I know that after I get the spiritual bread, the material bread will come." And I always see this happen: suddenly someone will come along and give me some money or food. And at that moment I thank God, and let others know all that God has been doing for me.

Marie Céres Marcelus offered these reflections near her home in Port-au-Prince, Haiti, in 1995.

Wipe Out Our Debts

Questions to Begin

10 minutes
Use a question or two to get warmed up for the reading.

1 Describe a time when someone forgave a debt you owed.

2 Describe a time when you forgave a debt.

10 minutes
Read the passage aloud. Let individuals take turns reading paragraphs.

The Focus

". . . forgive us our trespasses as we forgive those who trespass against us . . ."

The Background

The fifth petition concerns forgiveness. As Jesus guides us to ask God to forgive our sins, he reminds us that our seeking forgiveness from God is connected with our forgiving others for their sins against us. This point is so important that Jesus emphasizes it immediately after the prayer (6:14–15). Later, he repeats it in a parable (18:21–35). Jesus also teaches that if we seek reconciliation with God, we must make an effort to be reconciled with those against whom *we* have sinned (5:23–24). Thus, our request for God's forgiveness is tied up with forgiveness granted and forgiveness sought among ourselves.

The Reading: Matthew 6:9–15; 18:21–35

The Lord's Prayer

6:9 "Pray then in this way:
 Our Father in heaven,
  hallowed be your name.
10 Your kingdom come.
 Your will be done,
  on earth as it is in heaven.
11 Give us this day our daily bread.
12 And forgive us our debts,
  as we also have forgiven our debtors.
13 And do not bring us to the time of trial,
  but rescue us from the evil one."

Jesus' Commentary on His Prayer

14 "For if you forgive others their trespasses, your heavenly Father will also forgive you; 15 but if you do not forgive others, neither will your Father forgive your trespasses."

A Parable Makes the Same Point

18:21 Peter came and said to him, "Lord, if another member of the church* sins against me, how often should I forgive? As many as seven times?"

22 Jesus said to him, "Not seven times, but, I tell you, seventy-seven times.

23 "For this reason the kingdom of heaven may be compared to a king who wished to settle accounts with his slaves. 24 When he began the reckoning, one who owed him ten thousand talents was brought to him; 25 and, as he could not pay, his lord ordered him to be sold, together with his wife and children and all his possessions, and payment to be made. 26 So the slave fell on his knees before him, saying, 'Have patience with me, and I will pay you everything.' 27 And out of pity for him, the lord of that slave released him and forgave him the debt.

28 "But that same slave, as he went out, came upon one of his fellow slaves who owed him a hundred denarii; and seizing him by the throat, he said, 'Pay what you owe.' 29 Then his fellow slave fell down and pleaded with him, 'Have patience with me, and I will pay you.' 30 But he refused; then he went and threw him into prison until he would pay the debt. 31 "When his fellow slaves saw what had happened, they were greatly distressed, and they went and reported to their lord all that had taken place. 32 Then his lord summoned him and said to him, 'You wicked slave! I forgave you all that debt because you pleaded with me. 33 Should you not have had mercy on your fellow slave, as I had mercy on you?' 34 And in anger his lord handed him over to be tortured until he would pay his entire debt. 35 So my heavenly Father will also do to every one of you, if you do not forgive your brother or sister from your heart."

*Greek if my brother

First Impression

5 minutes
Briefly mention a question you have about the reading or one thing in it that surprised, impressed, delighted, or challenged you. No discussion! Just listen to one another's reactions.

If participants have not read this section already, read it aloud.
Otherwise go on to "Questions for Reflection and Discussion."

"Forgive us our trespasses . . ." Like the petition for bread, this one also expresses a daily need. Give us today our daily forgiveness!

Unfortunately, the traditional translation—"trespasses"— does not capture the meaning of the Greek very accurately. The Greek word here means "debts." While *trespasses* and *debts* are similar, they are not the same thing. Trespassing means entering someone's property without permission; being in debt means owing something to someone. As long ago as the sixteenth century, the Catholic scholars who produced the Douay-Rheims version offered a better translation: "forgive us our *debts*, as we also forgive our *debtors*" (Matthew 6:12; italics mine). By using the image of indebtedness, Jesus expresses a view of sin: it is a failure to repay a debt. But what does Jesus think is owed—and to whom?

On one occasion, asked whether people should pay taxes to the Roman government that ruled Palestine, Jesus pointed to a Roman coin, which bore an image of Caesar, the Roman emperor, and replied, "Render therefore to Caesar the things that are Caesar's." In other words, the money comes from the Roman emperor; if he wants some of it returned in the form of taxes, give it back to him. But, Jesus continued, render "to God the things that are God's" (22:21, Revised Standard Version). Now, of course, everything belongs to God. But one thing belongs to God in a very special way: human beings. Like the Roman coins that bore the image of Caesar, we, too, bear an image of a king—the image of our creator. Created in God's image (Genesis 1:26–27), we are to live in the world as reflections of his goodness, justice, faithfulness, and mercy. By doing so, we "render," or repay, to God what belongs to him, that is, ourselves.

Swiss Protestant theologian Karl Barth declared: "We do not owe God something, whether little or much, but our whole selves, for we are creatures sustained and nourished by his kindness." As Jesus put it, "You shall love the Lord your God with all your heart, and with all your soul, and with all your mind" (22:37). Since our whole lives are gifts from God, we should devote *all* our time, energy, talents, and resources to pleasing him. St. Thomas

Aquinas pointed out that it is only right that we should always do God's will in preference to our own, for to prefer our own will to God's is to fail to give God his due, to fail to pay what we owe him.

Our past failures to render our whole selves to God—that is, our sins—constitute a debt that cannot now be repaid. We have lost our chance to do God's will yesterday. We cannot go back to the past and choose God's will over our own. Any past unpaid debt of gratitude and service to God remains unpayable. All we can do is acknowledge the unpaid debt and ask God to clear the account. "Father, forgive us our debts."

Jesus' image of sins as unpaid debts highlights an overlooked dimension of sin. Sin is not only doing what we should not do; it is also neglecting to do what we ought to do. Sin lies not only in acts but also in failures to act. As expressed in the traditional prayer of contrition used in the sacrament of reconciliation, sin is both "what I have done" and "what I have failed to do."

While, by definition, sin is an offense against God, it usually involves other people, too. Here, also, Jesus' debt imagery is illuminating. It reminds us of our responsibilities to family, friends, and neighbors. We owe them our attention, presence, compassion, support, and so on. With them, too, we fail by omission as well as by commission.

To whom are we obligated? In his parable of the good Samaritan, Jesus makes it clear that our duty to love is not only to those who are close to us (Luke 10:25–37). He presents a symbolic portrayal of the final judgment (Matthew 25:31–46), showing that those to whom we owe assistance are simply those who need it. It is of crucial importance that the kinds of sin that this last-judgment scene targets are omissions—failures to give aid to the hungry, to the imprisoned, and to others in need.

In our relationships with other people, the impossibility of paying past debts is sometimes painfully apparent. We cannot return to yesterday and provide the dinner that a hungry person missed. We cannot retract the mean remark we made about another person, now that it has passed from mouth to mouth like an infectious disease. That person's reputation is damaged. We cannot restore the innocence and happiness of childhood to a man or woman whom we neglected or mistreated when they were young. Such debts remain eternally unpayable. But we can ask God to cancel them. "Father, forgive us our debts."

Of course, we are sincere in acknowledging our failures to meet our obligations only if we make a renewed attempt to meet our responsibilities, to *try* to repair the damage we have done, to seek forgiveness from those we have wronged. See Jesus' words in Matthew 5:23–24.

"As we forgive those who trespass against us . . ." These words might seem to imply that human pardon must come before divine pardon or even that our forgiveness of others makes us deserving of God's forgiveness. But Jesus' point is not that we must forgive others before God will forgive us; rather, we must forgive others before we can *ask* God for forgiveness. Forgiving others does not qualify us to receive God's forgiveness. Nothing gives us a claim on God's mercy. But if we refuse to forgive others, we disqualify ourselves from *asking* God to forgive us. "God's forgiveness does not rest on our forgiveness," explains French New Testament scholar Jean Carmignac. "But our prayer for forgiveness rests on our sincerity. Our prayer would be hypocritical if it were not preceded by our granting real forgiveness to others."

The imagery of debts continues to be instructive in regard to others' sins against us. Included in others' sins against us are sins of omission. We have all felt the effects of others' failures to carry out their responsibilities to us. When we were growing up, our parents and other adults in our lives were imperfect. Sometimes they were absent or did not guide or protect us. They did not teach us everything we needed to learn. Sometimes our employers, business colleagues, politicians, and others have let us down. Yet we must forgive all of these unpaid debts to us if we are to come before our Father sincerely and ask him to show us mercy that we do not deserve.

In the parable of the king and the two servants, Jesus takes the image of sins as debts and expands it into a story (18:23–35). A king discovers that one of his servants has run up an astronomical debt. He could sell the man and his family as slaves to recover some of what was owed, or he could put the man in jail in order to pressure the man's relatives to pay off his debt so as to secure his release. But the king forgives the man's debt, apparently for no other reason than that he feels sorry for him. Thus, the king symbolizes God. The servant's experience of the king's astonishing mercy, however, stirs no flicker of mercy in his own heart. He is ruthless toward a fellow servant who owes him a modest debt (equivalent to four month's wages for a farm worker). Through this story, Jesus delivers a sobering message: if you refuse to forgive others, you exclude yourself from the sphere of God's mercy. It is as simple and final as that. The parable stands as Jesus' own commentary on the fifth petition: Father, forgive our debts, as we forgive those who are indebted to us.

On this petition, Teresa of Ávila wrote:

I cannot believe that a soul which has approached so nearly to Mercy Itself, and has learned to know itself and the greatness of God's pardon, will not immediately and readily forgive, and . . . remain on good terms with a person who has done it wrong. For such a soul remembers the consolation and grace which He has shown it, in which it has recognized the signs of great love, and it is glad that the occasion presents itself for showing Him some love in return.

These are good words for contemplation by all of us who find it difficult to forgive.

45 minutes
Choose questions according to your interest and time.

1 When has the experience of God's forgiveness had a particularly strong impact on you? What was the impact?

2 What part does the sacrament of reconciliation play in your seeking and experiencing God's forgiveness?

3 When have you forgiven even though it was difficult to do so? What has been the effect of this forgiveness on you? on the person you forgave?

4 How can you tell whether you have truly forgiven someone for their sin against you?

5 In your experience and observation of life, what problems may result from refusing to forgive?

6 Many people find it hard to say, "Please forgive me." Why?

7 Jesus speaks about asking others to forgive us for our sins against them (5:23–24). How important is it to ask other people for forgiveness? How explicit does the request for forgiveness need to be?

8 What action could you take in response to Jesus' words in 5:23–24?

9 Looking back to question 5 in last week's session (page 47), what were you going to do to help someone else get the bread they needed? Did you do it? What was the result?

10 For personal reflection: Do you sometimes doubt whether God forgives you when you ask him for forgiveness? Reread and reflect on 6:14 and Romans 5:6–11 (where Paul speaks in terms of our being "reconciled" to God).

11 **Focus question.** How can a person recognize the sins for which he or she needs to ask God's forgiveness? How, in particular, can a person recognize sins of omission?

Prayer to Close

10 minutes
Use this approach—or create your own!

♦ Pray Psalm 51, asking
participants to pray the
individual verses in turn from
whatever translation of the Bible
each one has. Pause for silent
reflection. End together with the
Our Father.

Today's Examine

reemagining examen

Saints in the Making

Saved by the Our Father

This section is a supplement for individual reading.

By Helen Bloodgood

I had just finished buying groceries and was loading them into my car in the supermarket parking lot. As I got in my car, from out of nowhere, a man jumped into the rear seat, grabbed me by the neck, and demanded that I start driving. Stunned and scared, I tried to persuade him to let me go and take my car and jewelry instead. I might have saved my breath. "If you don't drive," he said in a cold, hard voice, "I have a gun and I'll blow your brains out."

I put my car into reverse as his grip tightened around my neck. I started to pray silently.

After a while, the man told me to stop the car. I hoped against hope that he'd just get out and leave, but he proceeded to strangle me. Then he dragged me into the back seat and attempted to violate me sexually.

I fought my attacker for close to twenty minutes, praying silently to God the entire time—*Please, help me. Please, help me.* Finally, crouched on top of me, brandishing a full bottle of liquor over my head, the man announced, "I'm going to kill you now."

As a child, I had been taught that I should pray at the time of death. What came to my lips at that moment was the Our Father. I started to pray it out loud.

"Shut up!" my attacker screamed. I invited him to pray with me. "It's too late for me," he said. I told him it is never too late with God. And again I began, "Our Father, who art in heaven . . ."

The man was furious and began shouting horrendous profanities. "I'm going to kill you!"

"Well, then," I told him, "I can go any way that I want. And I'm going to go praying." Pain was engulfing my entire body. With no strength left to fight, I closed my eyes and prepared to meet my dear creator. I began the Our Father for the third time.

Suddenly, the terror and pain vanished. I felt bathed in warmth and light, and a sense of peace flooded my whole being. It was the most beautiful thing I had ever experienced. *So this is the way it feels to die!* I felt an inexpressible joy as I continued to pray and waited for the blow to hit.

But nothing happened. Instead, I felt the weight of my attacker's body lifting off mine. I opened my eyes to find him sitting up with his head in his hands, trembling. After a few minutes, we somehow got into a conversation. Eventually, he got out of the car. I managed to call my husband.

I sustained serious injuries from the attack—four badly damaged discs in my neck and multiple contusions to my head, jaw, and ribs. But as I rode to the hospital with my husband and daughter, I knew that I had experienced nothing short of a miracle. I thanked God again and again for saving my life. I kept praying the Our Father. Every time I came to "forgive us our trespasses as we forgive those who trespass against us," I would hesitate. But I felt the Spirit tell me I must forgive my attacker. "Dear God," I responded, "you love this man as much as you love me. I forgive him. Please forgive him."

I won't pretend that I've had an easy recovery. To this day, I live in pain. My physical injuries have affected my work as a fitness instructor and seamstress. Fears and nightmares pursued me for a long time. Even now, not one day goes by that I do not recall the experience. Eight months after the incident, the man who attacked me was captured. Only then was I finally able to cry. God had seen me through those first eight months with his precious "daily bread." He now took my hand and led me through the trials that followed, as I sought out the professional counseling that was necessary for my healing.

My husband and I had a chance to talk to my assailant at his sentencing. He knows he is forgiven and that we pray for him. The attack and trial were highly profiled by the media, with every story mentioning the Our Father. Doors opened, giving me numerous opportunities to speak about prayer and forgiveness. I've also had the opportunity to meet with other women who have been sexually assaulted or abused. With my daughter, I have helped educate police departments on how to treat assault victims. With God's grace, our family has been brought closer together in our efforts to help others. How good our Father is!

Helen Bloodgood lives in Jupiter, Florida.

Keep Us from Sinning

Questions to Begin

10 minutes
Use a question or two to get warmed up for the reading.

1 When you're hungry, what do you think about?

2 Do you ever have trouble falling asleep? If so, what do you do?

Opening the Bible

10 minutes
Read the passage aloud. Let individuals take turns reading paragraphs.

The Focus

". . . lead us not into temptation . . ."

The Background

The sixth petition of the Lord's Prayer speaks of temptation. As we reflect on what temptation is and on what we are asking God to do about our temptations, it will be useful to consider two episodes in Jesus' life in which he experienced temptation. Although Jesus did not have any of the inner tendencies to sin that we find in ourselves, he was tested and tried by various temptations during his life (Hebrews 4:15). Matthew tells us that Jesus went through a time of multifaceted temptation just before he began his public ministry (4:1–11). And the Gospel writer shows Jesus, on the night before his death, wrestling within himself as he faces the most painful part of God's plan for him (26:36–46). Yet, at the very moment when he is dealing with temptation, he gives his disciples urgent advice about handling their own temptations.

Thus, the petition against temptation that Jesus gives us in his model prayer comes from his own human experience of the struggle to submit to God's will.

The Reading: Matthew 4:1–11; 26:36–47; 6:9–13

Jesus Is Tempted

4:1 Then Jesus was led up by the Spirit into the wilderness to be tempted by the devil. 2 He fasted forty days and forty nights, and afterwards he was famished.

3 The tempter came and said to him, "If you are the Son of God, command these stones to become loaves of bread." 4 But he answered, "It is written,

　　　'One does not live by bread alone,

but by every word that comes from the mouth of God.'"

5 Then the devil took him to the holy city and placed him on the pinnacle of the temple, 6 saying to him, "If you are the Son of God, throw yourself down; for it is written,

'He will command his angels concerning you,'
and 'On their hands they will bear you up,
so that you will not dash your foot against a stone.'"

7 Jesus said to him, "Again it is written, 'Do not put the Lord your God to the test.'"

8 Again, the devil took him to a very high mountain and showed him all the kingdoms of the world and their splendor; 9 and he said to him, "All these I will give you, if you will fall down and worship me." 10 Jesus said to him, "Away with you, Satan! for it is written,

'Worship the Lord your God,
and serve only him.'"

11 Then the devil left him, and suddenly angels came and waited on him.

Jesus Warns His Disciples against Temptation

26:36 Jesus went with them to a place called Gethsemane; and he said to his disciples, "Sit here while I go over there and pray." 37 He took with him Peter and the two sons of Zebedee, and began to be grieved and agitated. 38 Then he said to them, "I am deeply grieved, even to death; remain here, and stay awake with me." 39 And going a little farther, he threw himself on the ground and prayed, "My Father, if it is possible, let this cup pass from me; yet not what I want but what you want."

40 Then he came to the disciples and found them sleeping; and he said to Peter, "So, could you not stay awake with me one hour? 41 Stay awake and pray that you may not come into the time of trial; the spirit indeed is willing, but the flesh is weak."

42 Again he went away for the second time and prayed, "My Father, if this cannot pass unless I drink it, your will be done." 43 Again he came and found them sleeping, for their eyes were heavy.

44 So leaving them again, he went away and prayed for the third time, saying the same words.

45 Then he came to the disciples and said to them, "Are you still sleeping and taking your rest? See, the hour is at hand, and the Son of Man is betrayed into the hands of sinners. 46 Get up, let us be going. See, my betrayer is at hand."

47 While he was still speaking, Judas, one of the twelve, arrived; with him was a large crowd with swords and clubs, from the chief priests and the elders of the people.

The Lord's Prayer

6:9 "Pray then in this way:
Our Father in heaven,
hallowed be your name.
10   Your kingdom come.
Your will be done,
on earth as it is in heaven.
11   Give us this day our daily bread.
12   And forgive us our debts,
as we also have forgiven our debtors.
13   And do not bring us to the time of trial,
but rescue us from the evil one."

First Impression

5 minutes
Briefly mention a question you have about the reading or one thing in it that surprised, impressed, delighted, or challenged you. No discussion! Just listen to one another's reactions.

Exploring the Theme

If participants have not read this section already, read it aloud. Otherwise go on to "Questions for Reflection and Discussion."

The sixth petition presents us with a question of translation. The traditional translation speaks of "temptation." But the New Revised Standard Version speaks of "trial," or test. Now *temptation* and *trial* are similar, but they are not exactly the same thing.

When Scripture speaks of God subjecting people to *trials*, or *tests*, it usually refers to hardships or challenges that reveal their strengths and weaknesses. For instance, God tested the Israelites by leading them on a forty-year journey to see if they would trust and obey him (Deuteronomy 8:2; 13:3). God's testing has a constructive purpose: to spur our personal development and draw us closer to him.

By contrast, when Scripture speaks of *temptation* it usually means an attempt by some force to draw us away from God, either by luring us into wrongdoing or pressuring us to abandon what is right. Temptation involves an element of deception—a lie that sin will make things easier or better for us. Because temptation has the negative purpose of separating us from God, it never comes from God. Temptations come from the disordered aspects of our personalities, from sinful trends in society, or from evil spirits (Matthew 4:1; Mark 1:13; Luke 4:13; 1 Corinthians 7:5; 1 Thessalonians 3:5; Revelation 2:10).

The New Testament writers generally keep the concepts of *testing* and *temptation* distinct. James tells us that we are to welcome *trials* as part of God's dealings with us (James 1:2–4) but are never to claim that *temptations* come from God (James 1:13—although James acknowledges that God can use temptations to help us grow, see James 1:12). Like James, we also tend to distinguish between temptations and trials. If you lose your job, you might say that God is *testing* your trust in him. If a workmate suggests that you join him in a visit to an adult entertainment center after work, you might say that you are being *tempted* to fall into sexual sin.

Getting back to the Lord's Prayer—is Jesus speaking about *temptation* or *testing*?

To interpret the petition as a prayer against testing immediately raises a problem. James tells us that being tested is good for us. Why, then, would Jesus instruct us to pray not to be tested? The third-century theologian Origen noted that Jesus would be telling us to pray for the impossible if he meant us to ask the Father to preserve us from testing. "The whole of human life is a time of testing," he observed. "How then does the savior command us to pray that we might not enter into testing, when God tests everyone in some way?"

Origen's reasoning seems sound. It hardly makes sense to ask God to remove all earthly difficulties from our lives, and it seems very unlikely that Jesus would guide us to make such a request. Thus, we may accept the traditional translation as communicating Jesus' meaning. The petition is a request that God would not bring us into *temptation*, that is, into lures and seductions and pressures to abandon him.

But this raises another question. Aren't temptations just as inevitable as trials in this world? Is it possible to go through life—even with God's grace—without being tempted to sin? The answer, quite simply, is no. Temptations also are inevitable. But the petition in the Lord's Prayer is not a request that God would prevent us from being tempted. It is, to be precise, a request that God would not *lead us into* temptation. And in Scripture, *to go into* something often means *to become a part* of it and *belong to it*. For example, Jesus speaks about people *going into* the kingdom of heaven (translated "enter" in NRSV; Matthew 5:20; 7:21; 18:3; 19:23). He means *becoming part* of the kingdom, sharing in it, making it our home. Similarly, he speaks about sharing in eternal life as *going into* it (Matthew 18:8–9; 19:17), and he speaks about receiving God's approval as *going into* the joy of the master (Matthew 25:21, 23)—again, in these passages NRSV translates the Greek as "enter." Thus, to *go into* temptation would be to share in it, to become a part of it, a participant in it. The one who *enters into* temptation yields to it, hands himself or herself over to it. In short, to *enter into temptation* is *to sin*.

St. Augustine understood this. He wrote that "the prayer is not that we be not tempted but that we *be not brought into* temptation." As an example, he notes Old Testament Joseph, who "was tempted with the lure of adultery but was not brought into temptation" (Genesis 39:6–12). "It is the one who gives his consent to the tempter that *enters into* the temptation," Augustine wrote. Temptation is like a trap (see 1 Timothy 6:9). To *enter into* temptation is to fall into the trap, to get caught in it.

Thus, there is a very important difference between being *exposed to* temptation and going *into* it. When your workmate suggests an excursion to the adult entertainment center, you are being *exposed* to temptation. If you accept the invitation, you are *going into* the temptation. When the Holy Spirit led Jesus into the wilderness, Jesus was *exposed* to temptation (Matthew 4:1). But he did not *go into* temptation. That would be inconceivable!

In Gethsemane, Jesus tells Peter, James, and John, literally, to "pray that you not enter into temptation" (26:41, Revised Standard Version). Jesus is not urging the disciples to ask God not to be *exposed to* temptation. He knows that temptation is approaching them inexorably. Judas is about to arrive in the garden to betray Jesus. The disciples will then be severely tempted to abandon Jesus. The temptation cannot be averted or avoided. That is why Jesus urges the disciples to pray that they not *go into* temptation. He tells them, in effect, "Pray that you *do not yield to* the temptation to which you are about to be exposed." Unfortunately, as we know, they do not pray. When a wave of fear breaks upon them, they give way to it. They abandon Jesus. As he foresaw (Matthew 26:31), they *go into* temptation.

This helps us grasp what we are asking God for in the Our Father. We are praying that, when tempting traps are laid in our path, we would not get caught in them. We are praying that we would not believe temptation's lies or give way to its enticements or threats. We are asking him not to lead us *into* temptation.

And this leads us to a third and final question. Surely it is inconceivable that God would ever *lead* a person to yield to temptation. So why would we ask God not to lead us into temptation?

The answer to this question may lie in the original form of the prayer. Jesus probably taught the prayer to his disciples in Aramaic, the everyday language of first-century Palestine. In Aramaic, the petition probably had an ambiguity. It could be taken

to mean either, *"Do not cause us to go* into temptation" ("Please,
don't force us to fall into the trap of temptation") or *"Cause us
to not go* into temptation" ("Keep us out of temptation! Prevent
us from yielding to it! Make sure we don't fall into sin!"). Jesus'
disciples would have understood that he had the second meaning in
mind. His point, however, became less clear when the petition was
translated into Greek, and later into English.

So after all this examination of words, where have we come
to? Well, now that we can leave aside possible misunderstandings
of the petition, we can better grasp its meaning. In this petition, we
are asking God to protect us from turning away from him. We are
pleading with him to keep us from being separated from him. "Don't
let the lures or terrors of evil ever to draw us away from you!" In a
sense, we are saying to God, "Don't take your grace from us! Give
us your Holy Spirit to enable us to continue to do your will."

By praying this prayer, we acknowledge that we cannot
obey God without his help. Certainly, we must do our part: it is
up to us to choose to obey God. But by praying "lead us not into
temptation" we admit that our ability to make good choices comes
from him. "Having to ask not to fall into temptation reminds us how
weak and insecure we are," wrote St. Cyprian, an early bishop.

It keeps us from strutting about with our nose in the air, from
arrogantly claiming to be something we are not, from considering
as our own the glory of professing our faith or suffering for it. This
is why the Lord himself, training us in humility, told us, "Be alert
and pray not to fall into temptation; for the spirit is willing, but the
flesh is weak" (Matthew 26:41). If we start by humbly admitting our
need and ascribing all good to God . . . he will grant us in his loving-
kindness.

Cyprian put his life behind these words. With God's help,
he submitted to death rather than deny Christ, dying as a martyr in
Carthage (in present-day Tunisia), in the year 258.

Questions for Reflection and Discussion

45 minutes
Choose questions according to your interest and time.

1 What can we learn about dealing with temptations from the way Jesus dealt with temptations in the wilderness (Matthew 4:1–11)?

2 What can we learn from the way he dealt with temptation in the Garden of Gethsemane (26:36–46)?

3 Recently, when have you experienced God's grace helping you to avoid or resist temptation?

4 For personal reflection: When recently have you fallen into temptation? What lie did the temptation contain about what would make you happy? How did God provide help for dealing with the temptation? Did you take advantage of it? In the future, how might you deal with this temptation more effectively?

5 **Focus question.** What various means does God use to help us not to fall into temptation? What means of dealing with temptations do you find most helpful? What role do prayer and the sacraments play in your overcoming temptations?

Prayer to Close

10 minutes
Use this approach—or create your own!

♦ Pray Psalm 119:25–40, perhaps asking participants to pray the individual verses in turn from whatever translation of the Bible each one has. Pause for silent reflection. End together with the Our Father.

A Living Tradition

The Our Father in the Mass

This section is a supplement for individual reading.

Most of us would find it hard to imagine celebrating the Eucharist without praying the Our Father. Yet the Our Father was not always part of the Mass. On the basis of ancient texts, scholars conclude that it was not until the fourth century that Christians everywhere made the prayer a standard part of their celebration of the Eucharist. Why it took so long is something of a mystery. But the reason why they finally made the prayer a fixed part of the eucharistic celebration is clear enough. It had to do with their growing sense of awe at Christ's presence in the Eucharist.

According to liturgical scholar Robert F. Taft, SJ, in the fourth century "fear of unworthiness to approach the dread table of the Lord was a major cause of the abandonment of communion by the faithful." Thus, from the fourth century onward, the custom developed of laypeople refraining from Communion except on a few special feasts each year—a custom that lasted into the twentieth century. Against this tendency, however, the Our Father offered help and reassurance for receiving Communion.

In a sermon, St. Augustine, a bishop at the beginning of the fifth century, mentioned the practice of praying the Lord's Prayer before Communion. "Why," he asked his congregation, "is it recited before receiving the Body and Blood of Christ?" Answering his own question, Augustine continued:

Because human fragility is such that perhaps we entertained some improper thought, something came from our tongue that should not have, the eye glanced at something improper, if the ears heard some enticement they should not have, if perhaps such things have happened as a result of this world's temptation and the weakness of human life, it is wiped clean by the Lord's Prayer, where it is said, "Forgive us our trespasses," so that we might approach safely, lest we eat and drink what we receive unto our judgment.

Augustine assumed that the people in his congregation knew that if they had committed serious sins, they needed to seek God's forgiveness through the sacrament of reconciliation before receiving Communion. But he presented the Our Father as a means of obtaining God's forgiveness for run-of-the-mill faults and failings— and thus as excellent preparation for approaching the table of the Lord. His words speak to us today.

Opening prayer page 37
Closing prayer page 48

Week 6

RESCUE US FROM THE EVIL ONE

Questions to Begin

10 minutes
Use a question or two to get warmed up for the reading.

---

1 Do you do any gardening or grow plants at home? If so, what's the biggest challenge you face in getting your plants to grow as you'd like?

---

2 Have you ever been involved in a rescue effort—either as the rescuer or the one rescued?

Opening the Bible

10 minutes
Read the passage aloud. Let individuals take turns reading paragraphs.

The Focus

". . . but deliver us from evil."

The Background

A parable that Jesus tells during his public ministry (13:3–23) and a prayer that he prays at his Last Supper (John 17:15–23) will help us understand the final petition in his model prayer.

The Reading: Matthew 6:9–13; 13:3–9, 18–23; John 17:15–23

The Lord's Prayer

Matthew 6:9 "Pray then in this way:
    Our Father in heaven,
        hallowed be your name.
10   Your kingdom come.
    Your will be done,
        on earth as it is in heaven.
11   Give us this day our daily bread.
12   And forgive us our debts,
        as we also have forgiven our debtors.
13   And do not bring us to the time of trial,
        but rescue us from the evil one."

Various Responses to the Gospel

13:3 He told them many things in parables, saying: "Listen! A sower went out to sow. 4 And as he sowed, some seeds fell on the path, and the birds came and ate them up. 5 Other seeds fell on rocky ground, where they did not have much soil, and they sprang up quickly, since they had no depth of soil. 6 But when the sun rose, they were scorched; and since they had no root, they withered away. 7 Other seeds fell among thorns, and the thorns grew up and choked them. 8 Other seeds fell on good soil and brought forth grain, some a hundredfold, some sixty, some thirty. 9 Let anyone with ears listen! . . .

75

18 "Hear then the parable of the sower. 19 When anyone hears the word of the kingdom and does not understand it, the evil one comes and snatches away what is sown in the heart; this is what was sown on the path. 20 As for what was sown on rocky ground, this is the one who hears the word and immediately receives it with joy; 21 yet such a person has no root, but endures only for a while, and when trouble or persecution arises on account of the word, that person immediately falls away. 22 As for what was sown among thorns, this is the one who hears the word, but the cares of the world and the lure of wealth choke the word, and it yields nothing. 23 But as for what was sown on good soil, this is the one who hears the word and understands it, who indeed bears fruit and yields, in one case a hundredfold, in another sixty, and in another thirty."

Jesus' Prayer for Our Protection and Unity

John 17:15 "I am not asking you to take them out of the world, but I ask you to protect them from the evil one. 16 They do not belong to the world, just as I do not belong to the world. 17 Sanctify them in the truth; your word is truth. 18 As you have sent me into the world, so I have sent them into the world. 19 And for their sakes I sanctify myself, so that they also may be sanctified in truth.

20 "I ask not only on behalf of these, but also on behalf of those who will believe in me through their word, 21 that they may all be one. As you, Father, are in me and I am in you, may they also be in us, so that the world may believe that you have sent me. 22 The glory that you have given me I have given them, so that they may be one, as we are one, 23 I in them and you in me, that they may become completely one, so that the world may know that you have sent me and have loved them even as you have loved me."

First Impression

5 minutes
Briefly mention a question you have about the reading or one thing in it that surprised, impressed, delighted, or challenged you. No discussion! Just listen to one another's reactions.

If participants have not read this section already, read it aloud. Otherwise go on to "Questions for Reflection and Discussion."

"But deliver us from evil." Again we find translations in disagreement. The New Revised Standard Version says "from the evil one." This contrasts with the traditional translation: "from evil." A very literal translation of the Greek would be "from the evil." "The evil" suggests that Jesus has a particular evil in mind. What is it?

Later in Matthew's Gospel, Jesus presents a parable about a farmer. In it he speaks—literally, in the Greek—of "the evil" that snatches God's word out of people's hearts (13:19). That evil is obviously "the evil *one*," that is, the Devil. Thus, the Devil is probably "the evil" to which Jesus is referring in the Our Father.

It should not be surprising that Jesus' model prayer includes a plea for God to save us from the Devil. One of Jesus' first miracles was an exorcism, and he viewed his entire ministry and his death as a combat with the Devil (Mark 1:21–28; 3:22–27; John 12:31). He came to break the Devil's grip on us.

Why the "but" ("*but* deliver us")? The Greek word here could be translated "and above all." Thus, the last two petitions form a pair: "Keep us from giving in to temptation and, above all, rescue us from the Devil!"

The final petition does not imply that we are under the Devil's power. The Greek word for "deliver," or "rescue," here has the nuance of *keep away from*. We are not calling on God to liberate us from the Devil's domination as though we were still under it. Jesus has set us free. Rather, our prayer is, "Father, put as much distance as possible between that Evil One and us!"

The Devil works against us in various ways. Perhaps uppermost in Jesus' mind in this prayer are the Devil's attempts to deceive us, especially his attempts to deceive us into thinking that there is something better than God's kingdom. In his parable about the farmer sowing his fields, Jesus warns us of the danger that the Devil can deceive us on this point, preventing us from perceiving the true worth of the life God offers us (13:19). If we read the final petition together with the parable of the sower, the petition seems to be an appeal to God to enable us to escape the Devil's deceptions about the goodness of God and his kingdom. Jesus urges us to make God's kingdom our highest priority: "Strive first for the kingdom of God" (6:33). In this petition, we ask God not to let the Devil prevent us from doing exactly that.

Each year at the Easter vigil liturgy, Roman-rite Catholics renew their baptismal promises. To the priest's question "Do you reject Satan and all his empty promises?" the people respond, "I do." We make the same affirmation whenever we pray the final petition of the Our Father.

Many people disregard the Devil, even deny his existence. The Gospels stand as a reminder that the Devil is real—and is a force to be reckoned with (see Mark 3:11–12; John 13:2). Since in many ways he is more powerful than we are, he is to be taken seriously (1 Peter 5:8–9). But Jesus did not place this petition about the Devil at the end of the prayer to frighten us. Rather, this petition expresses confidence in our Father's protection against the Devil's deceptions.

St. Teresa of Ávila saw great value in trusting in God's protection as we travel the road toward heaven while maintaining a healthy concern about the dangers along the way. If we trust God, Teresa wrote,

we can travel along . . . in peace and quietness and not think at every step that we can see some pitfall and that we shall never reach our goal. Yet we cannot be sure of reaching it, so fear will always lead the way, and then we shall not grow careless. For, as long as we live, we must never feel completely safe or we shall be in great danger. And that was our Teacher's meaning when at the end of this prayer He said these words to His Father, knowing how necessary they were: "But deliver us from evil."

In this final petition, we are not asking God to remove us from the world, with all its misfortunes and suffering. God wants us to work for justice and peace in the world (5:6, 9), to be salt and light in our society (5:13–16). The final petition is not an appeal to God to beam us up off the surface of this distressing planet like characters in a Star Trek adventure. Nor is it a plea for God to shelter us from the world in a religious ghetto. Our prayer against the wiles of the Devil in the Our Father is like Jesus' prayer at the Last Supper: "Holy Father, . . . I am not asking you to take them out of the world, but I ask you to protect them from the evil one" (John 17:11, 15).

A final note. While it is useful to see that the basic point of the final petition is to ask God to save us from the Devil, we should not, therefore, narrow its meaning too much. In the Roman liturgy, after the Our Father, the priest continues, "Deliver us, Lord, from every evil." This brings out the full scope of the prayer: it is ultimately an appeal for God's deliverance from *every* evil. Recall St. Teresa's view, quoted earlier, that the Lord's Prayer has a broad meaning so that we can pray it in every situation.

Looking back over the whole prayer, we can see its structure more clearly than when we began our exploration. The first three petitions are parallel with each other: Father, may your name be hallowed, may your kingdom come, may your will be done. Thus, they form a threefold plea that God would accomplish his purposes in us and in the world—and a threefold commitment on our part to cooperate with him. The final three petitions also form a unit: forgive us our past sins, keep us from future sins, protect us from the Evil One who would lead us into sin. These final petitions are a threefold plea that God would draw us into total unity with himself—and a declaration of our desire to be rid of everything that would separate us from him.

In the middle of the prayer, we request our daily bread. We ask God for all the nourishment and help we need for our journey through this world into his kingdom, above all for the nourishment of Christ himself, who is God with us and for us.

Questions for Reflection and Discussion

45 minutes
Choose questions according to your interest and time.

1 In his parable of the sower, Jesus speaks about God's word being stolen from people almost without their realizing it (13:4, 19), of God's word failing to take root in their hearts (13:5–6, 20–21), and of God's word being choked off in their lives (13:7, 22). What illustrations can you offer of each of these problems in today's world? Which of these problems are you most vulnerable to?

2 Jesus also speaks about people who receive God's word and respond to it (13:8, 23). Who in your experience is an example of doing this well? What could you learn from that person?

3 How is God inviting you to respond to this part of the parable (13:8, 23) in your own life?

4 What are signs that a person has a realistic, healthy awareness of the reality of the Devil? What are signs of a morbid, exaggerated concern with the Devil?

5   When have you realized that you have undervalued something about God—his love, his forgiveness, his power, his holiness? What opened your eyes?

6   What message might there be for you in Jesus' prayer in John 17:20–23?

7   **Focus question.** Where do you experience a special need for God's protection from evil today? Is there something you should do to seek—or cooperate with—God's protection?

Prayer to Close

10 minutes
Use this approach—or create your own!

♦ Let someone read aloud the following thoughts on the Our Father by St. Cyprian. Pause for silent reflection. Allow time for participants to mention in prayer the needs of people they know or know about. End, naturally, with the Our Father.

We must not think only of ourselves. For we do not say, '*My* Father, who are in heaven' or 'Give *me* this day *my* daily bread'; nor does each of us ask merely that his own debt be forgiven or seek security against temptation and deliverance from evil for himself alone. For us, prayer is public and communal; and when we pray, we do so, not for one, but for the whole people.

Saints in the Making

Final Prayer

This section is a supplement for individual reading.

By Cynthia Cavnar

Father Joseph Kowalski had been ordained only three years when his pastoral work among young people attracted the attention of the German forces occupying Poland during World War II. The Nazis arrested him and sent him to the Auschwitz concentration camp.

Kowalski kept up a lively, clandestine ministry behind the barbed wire. "He gave absolution to the dying," a fellow inmate testified. "He strengthened those who were discouraged, uplifted spiritually the poor souls awaiting the death sentence, brought them Communion secretly, and even managed to organize holy Mass in the huts, as well as leading prayers and helping the needy."

On a particularly hot day in July 1942, a witness later reported, the guards were amusing themselves with acts of cruelty. They threw some prisoners into a cesspool and others into a muddy canal, then took a few who survived this treatment to a large, empty barrel which was lying on its side and served as a refuge for the camp dogs. "There they were compelled to imitate the dogs by barking," the witness said, "and then lick up from the ground soup that had been thrown down there to feed them." Before killing the prisoners, the head guard shouted, "Where is that Catholic priest? Let him bless them for their journey into eternity." In response, guards pulled Father Kowalski out of the cesspool where he had been thrown. Dripping from head to foot and driven forward by blows, he came to the barrel and was forced to get up on top of it.

Father Kowalski knelt and made the sign of the cross. Then, slowly and forcefully, he recited the Our Father, the Hail Mary, and the Hail, Holy Queen.

"The words of eternal truth contained in the divine phrases of the Lord's Prayer made a vivid impression on the prisoners," said an inmate. "We tasted the words of Father Kowalski as material food for the peace we longed for. We witnessed the sublime mystery celebrated by Father Kowalski against that macabre backdrop. A companion whispered in my ear: 'A prayer like that the world has never heard. Perhaps they did not pray like that even in the catacombs.'"

Later that night the guards drowned the young priest in the cesspool. In 1999, Pope John Paul II declared Joseph Kowalski "Blessed"—the final stage on the way to formal recognition as a saint.

Suggestions for Bible Discussion Groups

Like a camping trip, a Bible discussion group works best if you agree on where you're going and how you intend to get there. Many groups use their first meeting to talk over such questions. Here is a checklist of issues, with bits of advice from people who have experience in Bible discussions. (A planning discussion will go more smoothly if the leaders have thought through the following issues beforehand.)

Agree on your purpose. Are you getting together to gain wisdom and direction for your lives? to finally get acquainted with the Bible? to support one another in following Christ? to encourage those who are exploring—or reexploring—the Church? for other reasons?

Agree on attitudes. For example: "We're all beginners here." "We're here to help one another understand and respond to God's word." "We're not here to offer counseling or direction to one another." "We want to read Scripture prayerfully." What do *you* wish to emphasize? Make it explicit!

Agree on ground rules. Barbara J. Fleischer, in her useful book *Facilitating for Growth*, recommends that a group clearly state its approach to the following:

- *Preparation.* Do we agree to read the material and prepare answers to the questions before each meeting?
- *Attendance.* What kind of priority will we give to our meetings?
- *Self-revelation.* Are we willing to help the others in the group gradually get to know us—our weaknesses as well as our strengths, our needs as well as our gifts?
- *Listening.* Will we commit ourselves to listen to one another?
- *Confidentiality.* Will we keep everything that is shared *with* the group *in* the group?
- *Discretion.* Will we refrain from sharing about the faults and sins of people who are not in the group?
- *Encouragement and support.* Will we give as well as receive?
- *Participation.* Will we give each person the time and opportunity to make a contribution?

You could probably take a pen and draw a circle around *listening* and *confidentiality*. Those two points are especially important.

The following items could be added to Fleischer's list:

♦ *Relationship with parish.* Is our group part of the adult faith-formation program? independent but operating with the express approval of the pastor? not a parish-based group?

♦ *New members.* Will we let new members join us once we have begun the six weeks of discussions?

Agree on housekeeping.

♦ *When will we meet?*

♦ *How often will we meet?* Meeting weekly or every other week is best if you can manage it. William Riley remarks, "Meetings once a month are too distant from each other for the threads of the last session not to be lost" (*The Bible Study Group: An Owner's Manual*).

♦ *How long will each meeting run?*

♦ *Where will we meet?*

♦ *Is any setup needed?* Christine Dodd writes that "the problem with meeting in a place like a church hall is that it can be very soul-destroying," given the cold, impersonal feel of many church facilities. If you have to meet in a church facility, Dodd recommends doing something to make the area homey (*Making Scripture Work*).

♦ *Who will host the meetings?* Leaders and hosts are not necessarily the same people.

♦ *Will we have refreshments?* Who will provide them? Don Cousins and Judson Poling make this recommendation: "Serve refreshments if you like, but save snacks and other foods for the end of the meeting to minimize distractions" (*Leader's Guide 1*).

♦ *What about child care?* Most experienced leaders of Bible discussion groups discourage bringing infants or other children to adult Bible discussions.

Agree on leadership. You need someone to facilitate—
to keep the discussion on track, to see that everyone has a chance to speak, to help the group stay on schedule. Rena Duff, editor of the newsletter *Sharing God's Word Today*, recommends having two or three people take turns leading the discussions.

It's okay if the leader is not an expert on the Bible. You have this Six Weeks book as a guide, and if questions come up that no one can answer, you can delegate a participant to do a little research between meetings. Perhaps your parish priest or someone on the pastoral staff of your parish could offer advice. Or help may be available from your diocesan catechetical office or a local Catholic college or seminary.

It's important for the leader to set an example of listening, to draw out the quieter members (and occasionally restrain the more vocal ones), to move the group on when it gets stuck, to get the group back on track when the discussion moves away from the topic, and to restate and summarize what the group is learning. Sometimes the leader needs to remind the members of their agreements. An effective group leader is enthusiastic about the topic and the discussions and sets an example of learning from others and of using resources for growing in understanding.

As a discussion group matures, other members of the group will increasingly share in doing all these things on their own initiative.

Bible discussion is an opportunity to experience the fulfillment of Jesus' promise "Where two or three are gathered in my name, I am there among them" (Matthew 18:20). Put your discussion group in Jesus' hands. Pray for the guidance of the Spirit. And have a great time exploring God's word together!

Suggestions for Individuals

You can use this book just as well for individual study as for group discussion. While discussing the Bible with other people can be a rich experience, there are advantages to reading on your own. For example:

♦ You can focus on the points that interest you most.
♦ You can go at your own pace.
♦ You can be completely relaxed and unashamedly honest in your answers to all the questions, since you don't have to share them with anyone!

My suggestions for using this book on your own are these:

♦ Don't skip "Questions to Begin" or "First Impression."
♦ Take your time on "Questions for Reflection and Discussion." While a group will probably not have enough time to work on all the questions, you can allow yourself the time to consider all of them if you are using the book by yourself.
♦ After reading "Exploring the Theme," go back and reread the Scripture text before answering the Questions for Reflection and Discussion.
♦ Take the time to look up all the parenthetical Scripture references.
♦ Read additional sections of Scripture related to the excerpts in this book. For example, read the portions of Scripture that come before and after the sections that form the readings in this Six Weeks book. You will understand the readings better by viewing them in their context in the Bible.
♦ Since you control the pace, give yourself plenty of opportunities to reflect on the meaning of the Scripture passages for you. Let your reading be an opportunity for these words to become God's words to you.

Resources

Bibles

The following editions of the Bible contain the full set of biblical books recognized by the Catholic Church, along with a great deal of useful explanatory material:

- The Catholic Study Bible (Oxford University Press), which uses the text of the New American Bible
- The Catholic Bible: Personal Study Edition (Oxford University Press), which also uses the text of the New American Bible
- The New Jerusalem Bible, the regular (not the reader's) edition (Doubleday)

Books, Web Sites, and Other Resources

- *The Catechism of the Catholic Church*, sections 2759–2865.
- Romano Guardini, *The Lord's Prayer*, trans. Isabel McHugh (Manchester, NH: Sophia Institute Press, 1996).
- Teresa of Ávila, *The Way of Perfection* (any English translation), chapters 30–42.
- Tertullian, Cyprian, and Origen, *On the Lord's Prayer*, trans. and ed. Alistair Stewart-Sykes (Crestwood, NY: St. Vladimir's Seminary Press, 2004).
- Thomas Aquinas, *The Three Greatest Prayers: Commentaries on the Lord's Prayer, the Hail Mary, and the Apostles' Creed*, trans. Laurence Shapcote, OP (Manchester, NH: Sophia Institute Press, 1990).

How has Scripture had an impact on your life? Was this book helpful to you in your study of the Bible? Please send comments, suggestions, and personal experiences to Kevin Perrotta, General Editor, Trade Editorial Department, Loyola Press, 3441 N. Ashland Ave., Chicago, IL 60657.